FHM BACHELOR GUIDE

NEW ENGLISH LIBRARY

EDITOR: Anthony Noguera
ART EDITOR: Dina Koulla
PICTURE EDITOR: Laura Carlile
PRODUCTION EDITOR: Matthew Bingham
WRITERS: Martin Daubney, Flic Louise Everett,
George Halliwell, Gavin Newsham, Ben Raworth,
Andrew Woods
ADDITIONAL MATERIAL: Steve Farrell, Grub Smith
DESIGNER: Damian Wilkinson
PICTURE RESEARCHERS: Steve Nash, Regina Wolek
ILLUSTRATIONS: Justin Golby

First published by Hodder & Stoughton in 1998
A division of Hodder Headline PLC

The right of Emap Metro Limited to be identified
as the Author of the Work has been asserted
by them in accordance with the Copyright, Designs
and Patents Act 1988.

10 9 8 7 6 5 4 3 2 1

A CIP catalogue record for this title
is available from The British Library.

ISBN: 0 340 72868 X

Printed and bound in Great Britain
by The Bath Press.

Hodder & Stoughton Ltd
A division of Hodder Headline PLC
338 Euston Road
London NW1 3BH

The only book you should ever read…

CONTENTS

KOBAL, PSC, ADAM LAWRENCE

The multi-purpose wardrobe, page 78

Three minutes to live? Best drink up, then. Page 113

TENNENT'S Alc 9.0% Vol

She looks alright – but is she full of evil? Page 42

Tex "The Healer"
Grissom ended up
missing the gunfight

HOW TO DUMP YOUR GIRLFRIEND

When it's all over bar the shouting, are you a gentleman or a cad? Check your record against *FHM*'s ten methods to ending that beautiful affair

THE GOOD...

THE SMOTHERING GAMBIT
Method If there's one thing worse than a sinner, it's a saint. Kiss and cuddle her in public; keep staring into her eyes; make up a cuddly nickname for her.
Effectiveness Middling. Some women like 24-hour attention.
How you'll look Very good. And you'll come over as hard-done-by when you're dumped.
Rating 5/10

ASK HER TO MARRY YOU
Method Go down on bended knee and she'll analyse your personality down to the last detail. You're bound to come out looking bad – you're a man.
Effectiveness High. Just check first she's not desperate to get hitched.
How you'll look Noble.
Rating 7/10

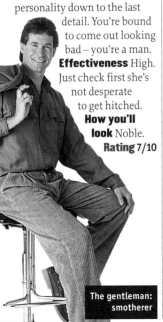

The gentleman: smotherer

GO ON SEPARATE HOLIDAYS
Method Send yourself post-cards and sign them with a kiss. And when you come back, have odd, laughter-inducing phone calls with "new friends".
Effectiveness Good. The paranoia can only lead to a split. And you get to go abroad.
How you'll look Poor. You'll be seen as the scumbag you are.
Rating 6/10

GO ON HOLIDAY TOGETHER
Method What could be simpler? Spend your time ogling other girls, act like a lout, criticise foreign cultures and refuse to eat anything except chips.
Effectiveness Extremely high. Arguments about maps, the weather, the people – all will lead to hatred and schism.
How you'll look You'll blend in with all the other idiots.
Rating 4/10

FIND YOURSELF
Method Sit around eating wheat germ, listening to whale music and refusing to pollute your body with alcohol and meat. Be reasonable all the time.
Effectiveness Superb. No woman with shaved armpits and a personality can stay with a man both sexless and creepy.
How you'll look Appalling. You'll lose all your friends as well as your woman.
Rating 5/10

...AND THE BAD

THE SLOB TACTIC
Method This is a great, as all the things you need to do are supremely enjoyable: increase your late-night, alcohol-fuelled poker sessions; pick your nose whenever you feel like it; fart out loud in public and laugh.
Effectiveness High. Your girl will soon sickened of you.
How you'll look Bad. You'll have difficulty getting another (clean) girlfriend.
Rating 6/10

FAX HER
Method Simply ditch the woman in your life with a scribbled electronic message. "Ta ra, pet," should do the trick.
Effectiveness Great. You avoid both the threat of physical violence and any verbal attempt at reconciliation.
How you'll look Rotten. You'll be labelled a coward. Rightly.
Rating 2/10

USE A THIRD PARTY
Method Slightly complex to engineer but well worth the effort. Have a friend sow the seeds of doubt in your girl's mind about your fidelity.
Effectiveness Middling. She might turn on the friend for spreading tales. Or she might cop off with him.
How you'll look Good. You can duly play the lover scorned when given the flick.
Rating 3/10

The cad: faxer

PACK UP AND LEAVE
Method An all-time classic. Only works for couples who live together, of course, and you should line up somewhere to go before chipping.
Effectiveness Cast-iron, unless you're with a simpleton who won't notice you've left.
How you'll look Who cares? You've gone, and you're free.
Rating 10/10

GET CAUGHT OUT
Method The Number One cause of splits: let your girlfriend find condoms in your jacket; work late and come home really happy; go off sex.
Effectiveness High. With the bonus of illicit pleasure while you wait to get caught.
How you'll look Pretty bad. But at least people will think there must be something up with her for you to have strayed.
Rating 8/10

KOBAL, REX

BED AND BREAKFAST MAN

Don't despair when the landlord starts hollering for this month's money. Here's a few ways to live rent-free...

The hoovering had to wait while Brad "rested"

MOVE IN WITH YOUR GIRLFRIEND Let's face it, you've probably been drunk and emotional enough to promise your lady the world and vice versa, so put the power of love to the test – move into her pad. Subtlety's the key: pass off your dire financial straits with a "don't worry, I'll sort it one way or another", then wait a couple of days. Next, add some severe trembling, twitching and – if your girl's mettle warrants it – weeping. Finally, throw in a "I just don't know what to do, the landlord phoned yesterday and..." in the hope she'll cut you off with an offer of a free bed. Alternatively, turn up at her place in the middle of the night with a bulging sports bag.

SLEEP AT THE OFFICE What could be more convenient than a city centre pad, close to work with amenities completely gratis? Yes, moving in at work improves punctuality *and* cuts down on bus fares. Personal possessions must be kept to a minimum – clothes, toiletries and tightly-rolled sleeping bag being enough. Your own desk is probably the best place to crawl under, as you can keep your personal affects close to hand and pop up bright-eyed when that annoying office brown-noser or the cleaner wakes you from your slumber.

THE THREE DAY-WEEK Stay at ten different friends' gaffs for three days each on a rolling monthly schedule. Simply ask to stay "just for a few nights – promise", then, after the third day, thank your host kindly, buy them a drink and move on. You'll never overstay your welcome and they'll probably feed you, too. And if the worst comes to the worst, camp out in a mate's garden for a few months.

THE ONE-NIGHT STAND If living in an office or a mate's place is infringing on your pulling possibilities, then worry no more. The one-night stand is the perfect rent-free kip: you get sex and breakfast thrown in and it won't cost you a fortune, either. Scrape up the entrance fee to the local meat market, feign drunkenness when *Move Closer* comes on at the end, and grab whatever's available. But do remember to take note of your girl's friends, as unwittingly pulling one of them on a future occasion may lead to awkward questions.

A FEW MONTHS IN HOSPITAL You've paid your National Insurance, so why not take a little R&R at the local hospital? Feigning illness is best, as breaking your leg could actually hurt. Try *faux* appendicitis – add a tiny amount of baking soda to some water, tighten the paste into a tiny stone and swallow. Then, clutching your lower-right abdomen, get yourself down to casualty. The pebble you swallowed will show up on an X-ray as a gallstone, which may be misdiagnosed as the cause of the appendicitis. Add a few histrionics and weeks of leisure and free scran are now yours. Just don't overdo it – they may decide to operate.

GET NICKED Embroil yourself in a legal wrangle (non-payment of rent, for instance), plead guilty and accept a fine. Normally you'll be given a term of repayment of, say, £10 a day over 20 days, or 20 days at Her Majesty's guest house. That's 20 days rent-free and no permanent criminal record, to boot.

FREE SEXY CHRIMBO TREE-TOPPER!

Whether it's a tinsel-limbed travesty or a gift from the people of Norway, make sure Emma's astride your tree

EMMA HARRISON
FHM CHRISTMAS ANGEL

FEEL THE BURN!

Why bother with the huge expense and massive effort of joining a gym, when you can do just as much in your very own home…

PHOTOGRAPHY: MICK HUTSON: STYLING: ISSY VIRDEN. CLOTHES AND TRAINERS: REEBOK.

THE ARMCHAIR DIP

Based loosely on the gruelling *Superstars* discipline of parallel-bar dipping, this variation of the event mastered by Judo black belt Brian Jacks requires all of the effort and none of the expense incurred in hiring complex gym equipment. Sit in an armchair with your legs lifted off the ground and extended fully; place both hands on the arms of the chair and slowly lift your yourself up until your arms are locked straight; lower yourself down and repeat 20 times.

THE TV SIT-UP

Turn the TV on just as *The Freddie Starr Show* begins, and lie on your back with your feet flat on the floor and your knees raised. Each time the son-beating scouser cracks one of his onerous "gags", lift yourself in traditional sit-up style. As you won't be doubled up with mirth, there should be sufficient exercise potential to ensure that a six-pack stomach is in place by the end of the series. Giving Freddie the double bird as you rise is an optional, and particularly satisfying, alternative.

THE BUTT-CHEEK ROLL

Those prone to outbreaks of flatulence should feel at home with this oblique-toning exercise. Sit upright in your favourite armchair and roll from one buttock to the other, in the manner of someone squeezing out a particularly stubborn fart. You can add a grimace or two for extra authenticity. Do this for the duration of each episode of *The Bill* for a month and you'll be sitting on buns of steel before you know it.

THE BUCKET FILL

If you're so bored that even the idea of washing the car seems quite appealing, take advantage of the situation by giving your biceps a thorough work-out. Once you've waded through the cellar to find your bucket, place it under the tap. Holding the bucket by its handle, slowly begin to fill it up. Keep the bucket as steady as possible as it fills, then pull it out of the sink when done. Repeat every time you need some clean water.

THE NEPHEW LEG LIFT

When your sister dumps little Jimmy on you for the afternoon and the brat sulks because you haven't got *Resident Evil 2*, you can both shut him up and keep your hamstrings taut with the Nephew Leg Lift. Lie on the sofa with your knees pulled to your chest, lure Jimmy into sitting on the soles of your feet, then lift the runt up and down until your legs can't take any more... or he falls over the back of the couch and catches his bonce on the bookcase. And if you don't have a nephew, try that old stand-by – the comedy dwarf.

KING OF TOOLBOXES

Nobody's going to try and pinch your parking space outside B&Q with this snuggled under the dog's blanket in the back of the motor. *FHM* selects the biggest, toughest tools known to man

PHOTOGRAPHY: PETER TILLEY. THANKS TO SNAP-ON FOR SUPPYING ALL TOOLS. FOR NEAREST STOCKIST: 01536 411011

When you were growing up, you probably didn't spend much time thinking about DIY. Why should you? It was clear that one morning you would wake up and magically find all those skills your father picked up had blossomed into your consciousness. Being handy with tools, you mistakenly believed, was genetic. The facility would evolve as you grew older, like facial hair.

Whereas you probably spent your youth playing *Donkey Kong* and *Defender*, your father put his time to much better use. In his teens, he was probably standing open-mouthed while your Gramps knocked up a garage over the course of a weekend, like the Amish building a barn – except the garage would come with sliding doors and functional windows. There was no dope-smoking and *faux* intellectual posturing in juice bars for your old man's generation: him and his mates got out there, hammer in hand, and made things. Things which lasted. Things which didn't fall off the wall when you put other things on top of them.

Maybe it all comes down to pride and the nobility of manual labour. The last time you felt any pride in an achievement was probably when you successfully worked out how to programme the video to record *ER* ten days in advance.

You don't believe us? Take a close look at your own hands. They're Fairy-soft and manicured, like a lady's. Remember those lumps on the palm of your father's hands? They're callouses, and they come from hard graft, from getting your hands dirty. Your father would sooner see another man messing with his wife than fiddling with his castle. Think about that the next time you need to call out the electrician to make the lamp go back on.

Snap-On orange screwdriver set
This range of screwdrivers with their lovely, ergonomically-designed handles won't raise welts on the palm of your hand every time you fix a plug.

Snap-On ¼-in to ¹³/₁₆-in socket set
Some men like to tinker with their cars in the front garden early on a Sunday afternoon. Now, with these spanners, taking all four wheels off has never been easier.

Snap-On high leverage pliers
If you get a really big splinter stuck in your finger, these are the boys to tug it out with. They're also good for working with badly hammered nails and wonky screws.

Bosch DUS 20 ultrasonic measuring device
If the standard tape-measure isn't gadgety enough for you, try this battery-powered baby. Point it at the wall and the digital reading comes up like magic, perfect every time.

Seven Drawer roll cab
That biscuit tin with a cottage on top you call a toolbox isn't fit for storing fishing tackle. You want this daddy of all boxes: it comes on wheels and has a proper lock. And it's postbox red. Beezer.

Snap-On ratcheting magnetic screwdrivers
A tidy sets of little devils, with nifty T-bar handles. If you're a clumsy git and often let your tools slip, at least the screw won't fall off the end of these magnetised gadgets.

Snap-On IM5100 high-impact wrench
Extracting fiddly, jammed-in pieces of metal can suddenly become like pulling teeth from a tramp with gingivitis – but only if you use this monster of a tool.

PDR5A Airdrill
Watch in wonder, tea-mug in hand, fag in mouth, as this mighty air-powered drill cuts through everything in sight with a banshee wail.

Snap-On QC Series micrometer click-type torque wrench
Who gives a shit what this thing does? Just look at the name. Tools aren't called anything better than this: all you have to do is memorise it and chuck it into the conversation next time you're down the pub.

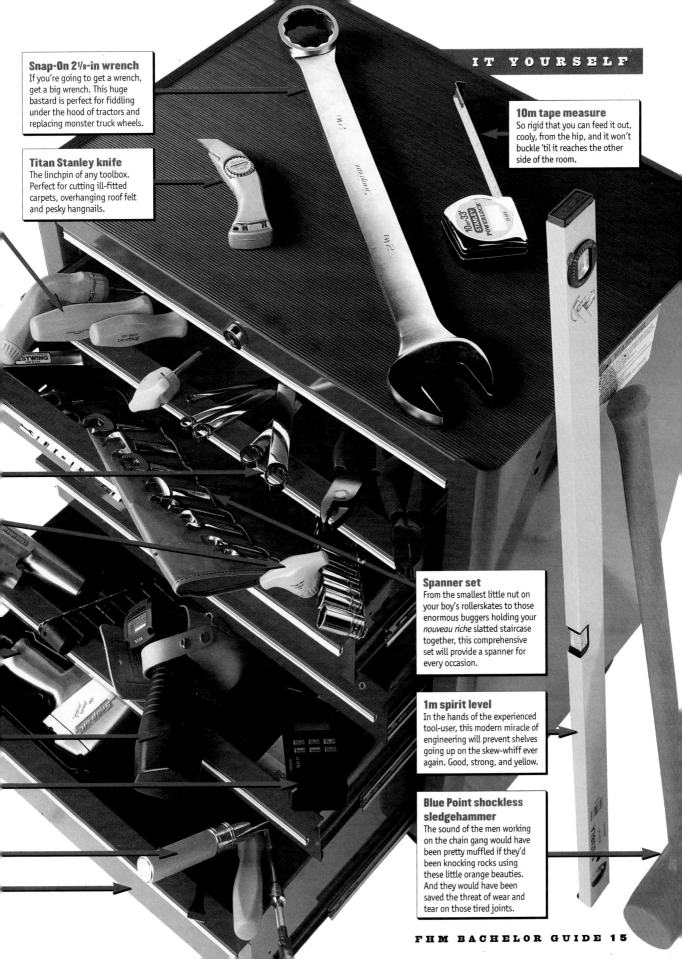

Snap-On 2⅛-in wrench
If you're going to get a wrench, get a big wrench. This huge bastard is perfect for fiddling under the hood of tractors and replacing monster truck wheels.

Titan Stanley knife
The linchpin of any toolbox. Perfect for cutting ill-fitted carpets, overhanging roof felt and pesky hangnails.

10m tape measure
So rigid that you can feed it out, cooly, from the hip, and it won't buckle 'til it reaches the other side of the room.

Spanner set
From the smallest little nut on your boy's rollerskates to those enormous buggers holding your *nouveau riche* slatted staircase together, this comprehensive set will provide a spanner for every occasion.

1m spirit level
In the hands of the experienced tool-user, this modern miracle of engineering will prevent shelves going up on the skew-whiff ever again. Good, strong, and yellow.

Blue Point shockless sledgehammer
The sound of the men working on the chain gang would have been pretty muffled if they'd been knocking rocks using these little orange beauties. And they would have been saved the threat of wear and tear on those tired joints.

DAD'S TOOLBAG

Revealed – your father's answer to nuts, nails, Formica and underfelt

The hammer The trusty hammer has three basic components: the head, the claw and the handle. Obvious duties include the hammering and retrieval of nails and the hitting of faulty electrical equipment, while its handle can be utilised for knocking loosened wooden joints.

The saw This thing cuts. And not much more. Essential when constructing or altering wooden furniture, the rubbing of a candle along its blade will increase its life and save on elbow grease.

The screwdriver This baby has more faces than Moriarty: the cross-head Philips, the flathead and the Alen among them. Not only will it let you fix two facing work surfaces together, it can also be employed in the lifting of paint-pot lids and common or garden de-grouting.

The stick A constant source of entertainment to Fido the builder's mate, and indispensable for stirring, prising and hitting things.

The power drill Although on the wrong end

CACKHANDED OFFSPRING

"I blame the teachers..."

Don't lie. At some point in your short life you have tried, with complete lack of success, to "improve" something around the house. Maybe you thought you would put up a nice set of shelves to hold your video collection. Armed with the latest drill and a snazzy plumbline you marked your wall-space out, prepared all the holes, and watched in horror as the first cassette brought the entire sorry mess crashing to the ground. Which is where it stayed for six months, until your dad came round for a bit of Sunday lunch and put the whole thing back in place, complete with a lick of varnish, in ten minutes.

The difference between you and your dad is that he really knows how to fix and make things. He actually enjoys the feel of sawdust in his hair and splinters in his fingers. You, on the other hand, enjoy ambling round the hardware store buying things, but when it comes to putting Rawlplug to plaster you're hopelessly inadequate. The reason behind this lack of skill is simple: during woodwork and metalwork lessons at school, the furthest you got was making a brush which lost its bristles and a hacksaw with no blade. Your father, due to a stonger work ethic and a pride in what he did, paid attention. Which is why you'll always have wobbly shelves and dirty windows.

Dad never came to terms with CDs

of public information films of the Seventies, the power drill can be the handyman's best weapon. Essential in the construction of shelving, curtain rails and the drilling of secret peepholes.

The file As Papillon will testify, given the choice of one tool the file is, frankly, unbeatable. Takes off sharp edges, smoothes down splinters.

The mallet This beast is the joist's number one enemy. Beezer at rectifying shoddily-asssembled flat-pack furniture, it's the equivalent to a snooker ball in a sock: it hurts, but it doesn't bruise.

The club hammer In close-quarter, hand-held smashing, the four-pound club has no equal. Can tear out an interior wall in seconds.

The Stanley knife Your good friend Stanley helps to cut carpet, correct ill-measured wallpaper and sharpen your HBs – which should be firmly wedged behind your ear.

The paint brush The humble brush can make even Grizzly Adams' shack look like Trump Towers. The icing on the cake, my friend.

The ubiquitous black bag Bung all your tools and rolling tobacco in this canvas holdall. An accessory you can guarantee will never, never appear in shades of "bitter chocolate".

"I had a cold the week we did shelves"

Test your skills

How well do you shape up to the old man?

You may think you're a bit of a handyman because you once assembled a "Björn" bedside table from IKEA. But when things really start to crumble around your home, does your hand instinctively reach for the phone? Go through our 20 common domestic dilemmas and see which of them you could fix unassisted, and which you would be bawling to your old man to come round and sort out – at maximum embarrassment to yourself. Simply tick the appropriate fixer after each question:

	You	Dad
1. Replace a 30-watt lightbulb	☐	☐
2. Change the fuse on a blown plug	☐	☐
3. Hang a picture. Straight	☐	☐
4. Unblock a sink	☐	☐
5. Mend a dripping tap	☐	☐
6. Replace a broken window-pane	☐	☐
7. Plumb in a washing machine	☐	☐
8. Make and put up shelves	☐	☐
9. Tile the bathroom (including grouting)	☐	☐
10. Paint a window frame. Tidily	☐	☐
11. Lay a carpet	☐	☐
12. Build a brick barbecue	☐	☐
13. Install an electric doorbell	☐	☐
14. Lay lagging	☐	☐
15. Unblock a toilet	☐	☐
16. Fix a burst pipe	☐	☐
17. Put in a cat-flap	☐	☐
18. Install strip/wall/ spot lighting	☐	☐
19. Build an MFI-style flat-pack wall unit	☐	☐
20. Replace a missing roof tile	☐	☐

The eagle had it in for Fingermouse

WHAT'S YOUR "DAD" RATING?

0-5 If you have ticked up to five "Dads", you are probably on the way to becoming a successful handyman, just like your pa.

6-10 You obviously paid some attention to what the old man was doing, but dozed off when the DIY got tricky.

11-15 You are very close to falling into the "Cack-handed Incompetent" demographic. Your dad will bail you out, but he's getting pretty bored, and ashamed, of his boy.

16-20 Just hope your pop doesn't die: not only will you be very, very sad, but you'll also run the risk of ending up living in a condemned building.

Alex was never alone with his paper friends

WALLPAPER FOR LOSERS

Everyone's bedroom wall has seen its share of posters. But be warned – they'll give your every secret away…

hilarious you blew up that snap from San Antonio. No one else in Christendom will.

POLITICAL STATEMENTS
Posters of multi-racial toddlers clasping hands in front of a mushroom cloud with the caption "Why?" suck. And battery hen/ slain fox/smoking beagle/ bunny-with-runny-eye posters will merely serve to make any potential conquest feel nauseous.

FANTASY ART
Women morphing into pseudo-erotic chromed motorbikes? No.

COMEDY BABIES
Kids with mohawks and leather jackets "giving the finger" have never, *never* raised a laugh.

FILM POSTERS
Ads for *Betty Blue*, *9 1/2 Weeks* and *Crash* are the last resort of the intellectual cripple.

MODERN-DAY ICONS
Pop up a poster of James Dean, Marilyn Monroe, Elvis, Humphrey Bogart, Che Guevara or Bob Marley and it will be painfully obvious that you are a living cliché.

STOLEN BAND POSTERS
Ripped from the Student Union wall, usually with at least one corner missing. Who gives a shit if you paid £4 (concessions) to see Dinosaur Jr in Mandela Hall?

ANYTHING FROM ATHENA
Posters of girls scratching their bare buttocks on the tennis court or muscular, oil-streaked men with abnormally large spanners in their hands mark you as a man with zero personality.

"MAGIC EYE" POSTERS
Stare at your wall for three hours hoping to see a migraine-inducing Statue of Liberty surrounded by leaping dolphins, or spend your money on beer? No contest.

SEX POSTERS
Sod those "naughty" twists on the Highway Code – "Warning: Humps Ahead!" – or amusing "condoms of the world" collections.

A LIFESIZE URINAL POSTER
Not funny *per se* – and even less funny if a pissed mate actually takes a slash against your wall.

ANY WILDLIFE POSTERS
A galloping horse, annotated: "If you love something, set it free. If it comes back, it's yours. If it doesn't, it never was," will not mark you out as a caring, sensitive soul. You will simply come across as a limp-wristed gaylord.

SPEED METAL BANDS
Surprisingly, a poster for The Stormtroopers Of Death's seminal *Speak English Or Die*, resplendent with a helmet-wearing, cigar-chewing skull, will not curry any favour with the opposite sex.

ANYTHING WITH A FERRARI IN IT
Especially Testarossas. They paint you as no more than a sad, day-dreaming, penniless adolescent.

DRINKING POSTERS
In truth, nobody *ever* laughed at a cartoon mouse slumped in an empty champagne boat, hiccuping: "I've got a drinking problem… two hands and only one mouth!"

CARTOON CAPERS
Hägar The Horrible, Snoopy and the contemptible Purple Ronnie were never, ever, remotely funny.

PAGE THREE GIRL/ PORN PULLOUTS
All women compare themselves unfavourably to other females – never more so than when they're naked. So while nudie posters may help your darting eyes tease out a slow wank of a Sunday morn, they'll make any woman's legs clamp shut in seconds.

MOONING SHOTS
You and the boys think it's

ARE YOU LONELY TONIGHT?

Try our quiz and discover the awful truth...

FRIDAY NIGHT

It's the last working day of the week, and money's not an issue. What do you do?

a) Join the gang from work on a booze-crazed knees-up in the centre of town.
b) Meet a few mates for a couple of pints down your local.
c) Invite an old friend round to your flat for a video and pizza.
d) Stare into the void.

CHRISTMAS

It's a snowy Christmas Eve. What are you looking forward to?

a) A fortnight's break in the mountains of St Moritz, skiing, drinking and swapping intimate presents with your pals.
b) A cosy day inside your warm country cottage, snuggled up in front of a roaring fire beside your best girl.
c) A nice day of reminiscing and sharing with close family and friends at your homestead.
d) Wrestling with the demons in your mind.

VALENTINE'S DAY

It's the most romantic day of the year. What do you expect?

a) A barrage of cards, presents and unrelenting carnal pleasure.
b) An intriguing unsigned card which puts a spring in your step.
c) An intimate and thoughtful present from your beau.
d) The excruciating drip of a leaking tap.

SUMMER HOLIDAYS

Work or college has broken up for a fortnight. What are you getting ready for?

a) A 14-day stetch of pina coladas, uncomplicated sex and siestas on the beach with the chaps.
b) A ten-day jaunt in New York City, visiting some old friends in their Manhattan loft.
c) Two weeks pottering around the beautiful fishing villages of Sardinia with your lady.
d) A 336-hour nightmare, curled up in a ball.

THE OFFICE DINNER AND DANCE

It's the big work shindig – the booze and the food are free and everyone's letting their hair down. You're...

a) Getting down to some dirty dancing with the hardbody from accounts.
b) Having a marathon snog and grope with several members of the typing pool.
c) Having a real laugh over cigars and port with your MD.
d) Wiping away a stream of tears with your napkin.

THE CUP FINAL

It's the big match, and your team are lining up in front of the Queen. Where are you preparing for kick-off?

a) At your pitch-side Wembley seat, your team's excited followers huddled around you.
b) At your packed local with a perfect view of the screen, beer and snacks by your side.
c) In your heaving living room filled with close friends, armed with lager and nachos.
d) At a "notorious" public convenience.

THE NEW MILLENNIUM

Everyone's booking their tickets for the party of the century. Exactly what have you got lined up?

a) A hedonistic, cliff-top bonfire celebration on the sun-drenched island of Java.
b) A fistful of exclusive tickets to a two-day monster bash in a millionaire's mansion on Crete.
c) A penthouse suite for you and your girl at Los Angeles' exclusive Hollywood Grande.
d) A bottle of Baileys and an evening's entertainment "live" with Noel Edmonds.

SCORING

MOSTLY "d" You know every square inch of your ceiling.
MOSTLY "c" You're nicely settled with your lady, but you could probably do with seeing your friends more.
MOSTLY "b" You're having a good time, but maybe you're missing out on the simpler pleasures in life.
MOSTLY "a" This is it, my friend – you're enjoying all life's pleasures to the full.

1998

FEBRUARY

Thursday 12 Week 7 · 043-322

8.00 WOKE UP. STILL ALIVE. NEVER MIND.
9.00 PUT COLD MILK ON MY CORNFLAKES. ATE THEM.
10.15 CLEANED MY BOWL. WENT AND SAT IN THE LIVING ROOM. IT'S RAINING. SO FAR MY HOLIDAY IS RUBBISH
12.30 CHECKED HOOVER BAG. IT WAS EMPTY. RANG THE WEATHER LINE FOR A WHILE.
4.00 HAD A CUP OF TEA. SEWED BUTTON ON MY SHIRT.
5.15 I'M GOING TO BED.

Friday 13 Week 7 · 044-321

6.15 – WOKE UP – THOUGHT I HEARD SOMEONE AT THE DOOR! FALSE ALARM – IT WAS A CAR DOOR SHUTTING
1.00 MUM CALLED. WE HAD A ROW. I HATE HER.
THE BULB HAS GONE IN THE BOG.
3.00 CHANGED THE BULB – THE OLD ONE WAS REALLY DUSTY. THINK I'LL HAVE AN EARLY NIGHT.

St Valentine Saturday 14 Week 7 · 045-320

4.15 WATCHED OPEN UNIVERSITY
* TAKE LIBRARY BOOKS BACK
1.20 WASHED MY SHEETS

Sunday 15 Week 7 · 046-319

7.00 WENT TO MASS - ONLY ME & THE VICAR TODAY.
1.00 HAD A NICE SUNDAY LUNCH AT KFC.

March Sun 1 | Mon Tue Wed Thu Fri Sat Sun 2 3 4 5 6 7 8 | Mon Tue Wed Thu Fri Sat Sun 9 10 11 12 13 14 15 | Mon Tue Wed Thu Fri Sat Sun 16 17 18 19 20 21 22 | Mon Tue Wed Thu Fri Sat Sun 23 24 25 26 27 28 29 | Mon Tue 30 31

SOMETHING FOR EVERYONE

"It's my favourite film!" your girlfriend exclaims. But that doesn't mean sitting through two hours of slush – if you know exactly when to wake up

PRETTY WOMAN

Okay, this film may be unmitigated nonsense, being the story of a tedious "love affair" between a Hollywood businessman and a whore who doesn't kiss (yeah, right!), but it does have its plus points. As early as the fourth minute you get a full eyeful of a scantily-clad beauty, and 22 minutes later there's another. You can happily snooze for the next half-hour, however, until the piano sex scene on the hour. You've then got to wait another annoying 30 minutes for the film's one and only nipple shot.
Rating 2/5. *Not great, but you do get ample rest between each bit of exposure.*

Pretty Woman: no kissing

little teasing due to the cameraman's refusal to show good honest angles. But the rest of the film's as limp as Robert Redford's hair.
Rating 3/5. *Quality scenes, but not enough of them. You can doze off after the first 15 minutes.*

AN OFFICER AND A GENTLEMAN

This is actually not that bad a film: it features suicide, martial arts and sex, although the women involved aren't exactly gorgeous and the nookie is little more explicit than most pyjama party tripe. In the first minute there's a buttock; sex in a car at the 40-minute mark; and one hour in there's a fairly decent session, even if it is in front of those rafia blinds found in hippy shops.
Rating 4/5. *A good movie, with enough carnal capers to keep your interest.*

An Officer And A Gentleman: bad blinds

FAME

There's not really much here for the seeker of the female form. There are two topless scenes in the 47th and 50th minutes respectively, but the bosoms involved belong to women you'd rather

Indecent Proposal: sex, cash, Vegas

INDECENT PROPOSAL

Demi might have looked like a muscle-bound whippet in *Striptease*, but she does do herself a few favours in the looks department in this soft-focus nightmare of a film. The fifth minute, no less, sees her writhing on the kitchen floor with Woody Harrelson; and nine minutes later she's slithering around again, only this time she's covered in lovely loot on a Las Vegas bed. Great scenes, although a

Fame: watch with the sound off

see covered up. There's one more topless shot just under two hours in, but Irene Cara cries all the way through it – she's being exploited by a dodgy photographer, apparently.
Rating 1/5. *Too many blokes in leotards dancing around the streets to wimp rock, and the women are on the dodgy side.*

ABOUT LAST NIGHT

It's Demi Moore again, although this time round it's the younger (and considerably less endowed) model. The film itself is twee, but there are some funny scenes – basically all the ones where Jim Belushi quizzes the mega-sickly Rob Lowe about his sex life. The 30-minute mark sees the first bra-strap, which is followed two minutes later with bath sex. Another bra parades on screen at 35 minutes, while exposed nipples peek out coyly after 48 minutes.
Rating 4/5. *The first hour is nicely punctuated with flesh, tailing off in the second half.*

About Last Night: set watch alarms for 32mins

SOUNDS OF SEDUCTION

Setting the mood is all important when you get the girl of your dreams back to your place. So spin any of these albums and you'll reap real rewards...

Barry made sure
his pool was kept
verruca-free

BEST FOR A FIRST DATE
Barry White – The Collection
THE GOOD NEWS Barry's tops when it comes to lurve. She'll be champing at the bit within the hour.
THE BAD NEWS Whacking big Baz on the stereo when you're in the mood for action is about as subtle as getting your old fella out.
SONG TO AVOID Girls, being girls, will ask you whether you're their "first, last and everything". Your reply could ruin her evening.
What not to say to her *"Forget Barry – you're my walrus of love!"*

BEST FOR A QUICKIE
The Buzzcocks – Going Steady
THE GOOD NEWS These catchy pop songs are ideal for a knee-trembler in the kitchen while she's hunting for chocolate biscuits in the larder.
THE BAD NEWS Pete Shelley's warbling singing style is as likely to induce a workable erection as tuning into the Shipping Forecast.
SONG TO AVOID *What Do I Get?* She's performed a sex act on you, you've dozed off, this comes on and she asks that very question. Hit the eject – and quick.
What not to say to her *"You're turning me into an Orgasm Addict!"*

BEST FOR DINING
Simply Red – Stars
THE GOOD NEWS Every girl likes Simply Red – they adore ginger Mick's velvety smooth vocals.
THE BAD NEWS Blokes find ginger men utterly offensive: one note of this gaylord's voice is likely to make you throw your dinner up.
SONG TO AVOID *Babies* – bad song; really bad topic.
What to not say to her *"Hucknall's generous donations to New Labour show he's never lost touch with his working-class roots."*

BEST FOR SHAGGING
Prince – Sign O'The Times
THE GOOD NEWS Prince, "Symbol", whatever he calls himself, is in the 100 Shortest Men In America list, proving that even a midget can be a hit with the ladies.
THE BAD NEWS This big old double LP will set you back some £25.
SONG TO AVOID The title track begins with the line: "In France, a skinny man died of a big disease with a little name..." Hardly the kind of thing you want to think about when you're on the job.
What not to say to her *"I sometimes wear heels like Prince. They make me feel more confident."*

BEST FOR A NIGHT-CAP
Massive Attack – Protection
THE GOOD NEWS Aside from the sublime, laid-back rhythms, the very title of the album is a much-needed reminder to wrap that little rascal later in the evening.
THE BAD NEWS Apparently, this LP is best appreciated while using what young people refer to as wacky baccy. Too much, however, and you'll feel more like eating an entire Swiss roll than jumping straight into the sack.
SONG TO AVOID Any tracks with big-chinned Tracey Thorn from Everything But The Girl. Put any thought of her jutting jaw out of your mind as you move closer...
What not to say to her *"Who'd have thought a bunch of straw-chomping yokels from Bristol could make music like this."*

BEST FOR SHOWING OFF
Phillip Glass – Music In 12 Parts 1&2
THE GOOD NEWS Minimalist, pseudo-intellectual nonsense that will impress any girl who finds pop music banal.
THE BAD NEWS This racket will drive you fucking nuts.
SONG TO AVOID The whole interminable mess, honestly.
What not to say to her *"The way Glass contracts rythmic figures in a stable diatonic framework somehow detracts from the music's dramatic structure."*

RETNA

"Don't let the bed-bugs bite," generations of moms have said to weary-eyed offspring. Forget the bed, Missus – the whole house is crawling with filth!

HOUSE OF

Living room Goodies on offer include the sofa (stuffed with food-matter and coinage), light (loved by gnats) and pets. The fact that cats and dogs mill about the sitting room means it plays host to the sort of micro- and macro-scum that likes nothing better than to jump from dumb animals onto you. Another living room lout is the silverfish. Not a fish at all but a repugnant antennaed thing, the silverfish loves paper. Oh yes, he could be munching through this very book. There's also the chance of "super-termites" if you've got wooden doors, beams and skirting.
The evil ones *The flea, louse, silverfish and termite.*

HORRORS

Bathroom Oh my Lord! Faeces, urine, tampons and dirt – all in the same room. The shower is home to damp, the bath encrusted in filth, the toilet the portal to Hell, while foul cholera loiters in water tanks and pipes. Some UK residents have spotted a Stateside cousin, the drainfly. This sick fuck gobbles up urine then pukes it out – ready to be lapped by the cat. **The evil ones** *The water fluke, cholera and drainfly.*

Kitchen There's no room more appetizing to creepy-crawlies than the kitchen – a veritable smorgasbord of decaying veg and meat and a banquet to evilness. The landlord of the kitchen is the housefly, which can drop close to 2,700 eggs in 30 days. Black specks on the walls? That's its faeces. And as for the innocent dishcloth, it's a festering seedbed of bacteria. **The evil ones** *The housefly, cockroach and roundworm.*

Bedroom Next time you're frolicking with a lady in your bed, imagine millions of lice gorging on your semen stains. Then picture those same lice hopping into your thatch for a good night's sleep. Another lover of your chamber is the earwig. And of course, anywhere where there's clothes and carpets is sure to have the moth and millipede pottering around. **The evil ones** *The crab, earwig, moth, millipede, lice and tick.*

THE ALL-PRO BUG FEST

Ladies and gentlemen – take your seats for The Battle Of The Bugs.
It's open to anything that flies, crawls or seeps, so let the antennae fly!

FIRST ROUND

Ant vs silverfish
The silverfish has no sooner left his corner than the ant comes in, mandibles first. A right-hand flick at the silverfish has it stunned, a second southpaw swipe flips it over. The ant stands proudly over the bug before cleaving its head off.

Bed-bug vs earwig
The microscopic bed-bug sinks its teeth into the earwig's skin, but the earwig is wise to this and flicks it off with a twitch of its strong rear haunch. The earwig then unwittingly treads on the bug as it tries to locate its foe. Safely through.

Housefly vs flea
Using his powerful rear legs, the flea aims a couple of flighted kicks at the skirting fly, which can only reply by spitting saliva. But when the spit from the cowardly fly dries up, the flea goes in hard at the winged one's feeble abdomen. The fly drops; the flea tries a body-splash; the flea is victorious.

Millipede vs daddy long-legs
The daddy plays the waiting game here, dancing round the millipede Sugar Ray-style. The only problem is that the long-legs' glances are far too slight. And the millipede has an ace up its sleeve: standing on its numberless limbs, the millipede rears up and crashes into the glorified gnat. The millipede books a place in the next round.

SEMI-FINALS

Ant vs flea
There are over 1,000 varieties of flea in the world, but it seems that not a one of them is a match for the mighty ant. The plucky flea has another problem: it can only live for seven days. But this bitterly-fought semi lasts nowhere near so long, as the ant pins the flea with his awesome mandibles and slices the bloodsucker in two.

Millepede vs earwig
These two are a similar height, and the earwig noted the millipede's "up 'n' over" during the previous fight. And as sure as eggs are eggs, the many-legged one flips up again – oblivious to the earwig's powerful pincers. The earwig gouges out the millipede's abdomen and waits for it to fall. It even takes off a few of its legs for fun. The final awaits, Mr Wig…

THE FINAL

Ant vs earwig
The ant goes in early doors and has the earwig on its back legs. Then disaster strikes for the hardy soldier, as one of its left hooks is successfully blocked by the earwig, which retaliates with a sucker punch, knocking the ant onto its side. But cheered on by its fans, the ant gets angry and dives upon the earwig's back. The earwig desperately pivots as its co-driver slowly pulls its limbs off, one by one. Soon the earwig lies motionless, while the ant rears up for its final victory gouge. The ring is flooded with the ant's fans, who dispense with the traditional champagne and eat what's left of its opponent.

The ant: a veteran, but overconfident?

The earwig: fighting above its weight

Ants: hard

RULES OF STYLE WITH DIGBY CRESCENT

Listen and learn as Digby wades through your queries...

Dear FHM,

I've recently had trouble with a swarm of bluebottles that's taken residence in my outhouse. The flies keep me awake at night with their humming and I'm scared to invite friends round for dinner, lest they should observe my verminous lodgers. The blue-bottles are a nuisance, for sure, but I believe that it's against the law to kill them. If that's the case, what should I do?

It is indeed illegal – in European law – to kill a housefly if it has caused you no physical injury or discomfort. But as noise is considered a serious problem, it is permissible to lead the flies away from your land. Simply strap a few raw steaks to a neighbour's shed and watch your winged pals vacate both your property and your life.

THE WONDER OF WINE

Leave that bottle of Thunderbird on the shelf and take your first steps into the magnificent world of the grape...

AFTER MONTHS OF PHONE calls, e-mails and a bit of stalking, you've finally persuaded her to have dinner with you. Once you've selected the perfect restaurant for the occasion, it's important to choose the right wine to accompany the meal. Remember, ask for Blue Nun or Black Tower and you've blown it. Worse, she'll probably throw the stuff in your face on her way out.

Starters If the starter menu leaves you cold and you're forced to order the melon, then liven it up with a drop of Madeira. If you go with the prawns, mussels or anything else plucked helplessly from the ocean, then an Alsace Riesling will go down quicker than one of Branson's flimsy balloons. Soup dullards may want to try a sherry if they really feel like pushing the boat out – but then again, they'll probably play safe with a Liebfraumilch.

Oysters and shellfish As the Chablis vineyards actually lie on ancient oyster beds, it will come as no surprise that a Chablis is a perfect accompaniment to these slurpy shelled critters. Combine the two and she'll be back at your place in less time than it takes Ollie Reed to decide on one for the road.

Chablis: brother to the oyster

1996

Roast dinners and game
The rule of thumb here is that the heartier the meal, the fuller the wine. So if it's pheasant, roast beef or roast chicken for dinner, demand an expensive Burgundy – and if she harbours any doubts about red wine with chicken, pour her a glass and await her apology.

Fish So-called demi-veggies – those non-meat eaters who occasionally dabble in "a bit of fish" – are on the rise, so if you end up sat opposite one and she plumps for the halibut, scan the wine list for an Australian or New Zealand Sauvignon Blanc. For a richer fish dish, try a Chardonnay.

Red meat Gorging yourself on bloody red meat can be a truly sensual experience, and is best accompanied by a full-bodied red wine. If there's a Bordeaux/Cabernet Sauvignon or a Burgundy/Pinot Noir available, you won't go far wrong.

Dessert Sweeter dessert wines, like a German Eiswein, may be lower in alcohol than port or a drop of single malt – but believe it, they're still

Sauvignon Blanc: fish-orientated

worth a guzzle. And as they're generally cheaper than a spirit, you should have enough cash left to grab a four-pack of Stella on your way home.

Cheese Cheese and wine are a perfect combination, assuming you're not a teetotal vegan. With traditionally popular English cheeses like Cheshire and Cheddar, go for a Claret or a Burgundy; with more potent Stilton and Roquefort, order a Rioja or a Côtes des Rhone. However, if you reckon you're in with a shout of some action, skip the cheese and call a cab.

Rioja: friend to cheese

The vin challenge

You probably think that people who go to wine-tasting sessions are all pompous old men who cover up poor social skills and a lack of wit with meaningless descriptions of wines they haven't even got the good sense to swallow. And you'd be right. Even renowned winetaster Michael Broadbent admits in his *Pocket Guide To Winetasting* that the practice of note-taking while tasting wine "can turn into a fetish". Nevertheless, the idiotic ramblings of wine bores does allow the rest of us to have a good laugh at their expense.

We've waded through two top guides – *Food And Wine Magazine*'s *Official Wine Guide 1998* by Stephen Tanzer, and *Wine Magazine*'s *Pocket Wine Buyer's Guide 1998*, published by Dorling Kindersley – and picked out their choice musings on five different wines. Then for each bottle we've added a fabricated description of our own. Can you spot which are made up? To keep you on your toes, we've

The lads loved to come round and frolic in Gazza's pool

also added one vintage of our own making and dreamed up three ludicrous descriptions for it.

1. Penfold's Cabernet Sauvignon (Australia)

a) "Minty, mulberry nose. Hints of chocolate with a concentrated palate of well-structured fruit and dense tannins."

b) "Well-balanced nose with a tinge of mould, layered with a tang of old clover. Tart, but flabby on exit."

c) "Lush on entry, then rather closed in the middle. Multi-faceted nose combines blackberry, roasted coffee, smoked meat and lead pencil."

2. Charles Heidsieck Brut Champagne 1985 (France)

a) "Very pale. Big,

"Sod this, I'm going for a pint of Heavy"

rich and creamy in the mouth. Caramel and toast flavours open nicely on the finish."

b) "A rich, generous nose leads on to a palate of biscuit flavours and a ripe finish."

c) "Veiny purple sheen. A fine, fat nose with yeasty undertones. Hot, robust finish."

3. Clos Malverne Cabernet Sauvignon (SA)

a) "A flinty, earthy nose; round and complex with a light and flowery aftertaste. Nicely satisfying, but effeminate."

b) "Thick and truffley in the mouth; harmonious and silky. Really loaded with fruit, and complicated by a vegetal nuance."

c) "A good nose showing brambles and white pepper, following through to a spicy palate."

4 Grand Vin de Chateau Marillion (Belgium)

a) "Carroty – a suggestion of damp earth. Earnest, if a touch overbearing. Hint of tobacco on entry."

b) "Brooding and lachrymose in the bottle. Bouncing and strident in the glass. Terribly shy."

c) "A rich, meaty nose and triumphant body. Mouth-filling fruitiness doesn't overshadow strains of strawberry *chemin de fer*. Slow off the mark, but a very strong finisher."

5. Beringer Private Reserve Chardonnay (US)

a) "Complex aroma of lime, charred oak, game and spices. Maintains shape to long aftertaste."

b) "Full-bodied, with a beautiful concentration of fruit on the palate and rich, creamy aromas."

c) "A tannic, perhaps even *satanic* preamble, showing strong, stalky thrusts. Pumping and luscious over ulcers."

6. Ramos-Pinto Duas Quintas Vinho Tinto (Portugal)

a) "Silky yet bright in the mouth, with good stuffing and firm framing acidity. Finishes fresh and persistent, with a note of white pepper."

b) "Refreshing, big and baked. Cocksure after-taste goes on and on and on. A little retarded."

c) "Rich and powerfully built with its melange of dark berry and cherry fruits. Spicy backbone."

THE TRUTH

1 a) Genuine (DK) b) Fake c) Genuine (ST). 2 a)
Genuine (ST) b) Genuine (DK) c) Fake. 3 a) Fake
b) Genuine (ST) c) Genuine (DK). 4 Totally made up.
5 a) Genuine (ST) b) Genuine (DK) c) Fake.
6 a) Genuine (ST) b) Fake c) Genuine (DK).

WORLD OF

The last time you locked yourself out, stubbed your toe or scraped your car against the garage wall, you probably cursed yourself as the world's biggest idiot. But you've a way to go – check out the ten greatest fools of all time

Junkie approaches undercover cop...

01:03:35:20

from two wooden pallets. After 14 hours of frantic paddling, he fell asleep on his makeshift craft, and was later picked up by a passing oil tanker. "If it hadn't been for that ship, I would have made it," said Tervit, somewhat ungratefully.

Shoplifter Barry Quemby's raid on a fishmonger in Boston, Massachusetts, was not carefully thought out. Deciding he fancied fresh lobster for dinner, Quemby stuffed two live crustaceans down his trousers and nonchalantly strolled towards the exit. However, agitated by their sudden change of surroundings, the lobsters duly panicked and began hacking away at Quemby's private parts. Screaming in agony, the robber plunged headfirst into a stand of tinned pilchards. Such was the ferocity of the lobster attack that Quemby's penis was severed, and had to be surgically reattached in hospital on the way to the cells.

TCR 01:04:27:16

TCR 01:03:53:

...and is arrested. Time elapsed: 52secs

When impoverished Brazilian maid Maria Benoiza Nascimento won $60,000 on the country's national lottery, she was delighted. But after her local minister told Nascimento she would burn in Hell if she ever tried to claim her prize – despite the fact that it would enable her to afford medical treatment for her three pneumonia-ridden children – the terrified maid duly set fire to the winning ticket in the course of an Assembly of God church meeting. Her fellow worshippers watched on, chanting: "Burn, burn, burn."

...strikes a deal for his "shit"...

Although determined to return to Britain after a fruitless search for work on the continent, 46-year-old Lawrence Tervit couldn't afford a ferry ticket home. Racking his brains, he hit upon the idea of sailing across the Channel on a raft built

During a bout of terrible toothache, Turkish farmer Ismail Ayyildiz went on a massive drinking spree to relieve his pain. Unfortunately, even when drunk, the farmer's suffering proved intolerable. Announcing to his friends that he was going to get rid of the offending molar there and then, Ayyildiz took out a gun and blasted his tooth. The bullet ricocheted off his dentition and into his brain, killing him instantly.

STUPID

6 Officers from a San Francisco narcotics squad were busy busting an addict who'd unwittingly bought drugs from an undercover cop when another junkie approached the undercover policeman, apparently oblivious to the fact that there were now several uniformed officers and a prowl car on the scene. He demanded cocaine, which the incredulous officer duly sold him before having the man arrested.

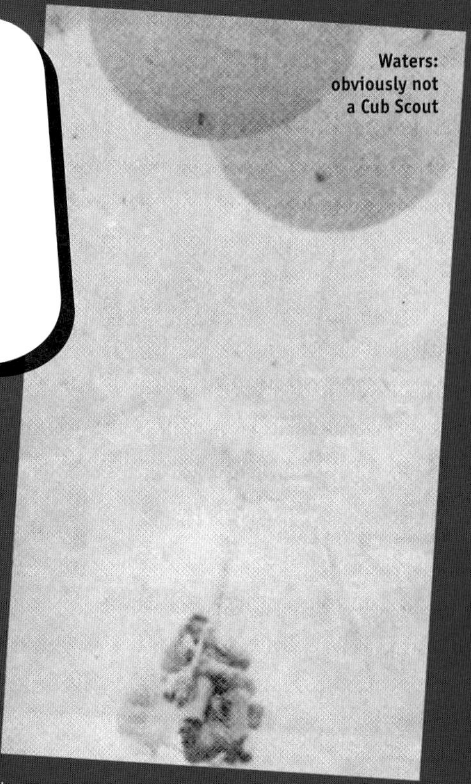

Tervit: ungrateful

5 Unnecessarily macho behaviour did for Pennsylania resident Carl Buxton. Buxton was enjoying a drink with his mates in a bar when he was bitten by a cobra. He ignored his companions' advice to go to hospital and kept on drinking. "I'm a man, I can handle it," he bragged. One hour later, he dropped dead.

4 Seventeen Americans from the Seventh Day Adventist church perished after hurling themselves into crocodile-infested waters during a religious festival in Tanzania. During a break, the Yanks were enjoying a boat ride on Lake Victoria when a party of youths on a passing cruiser heard the group singing hymns, and suggested they should walk on water like their saviour. Responding "Hallelujah!", 17 of them jumped into the lake. Most of the bodies were never recovered.

3 Nineteen-year-old Robert Ricketts was rushed to hospital in Bowling Green, Ohio after being struck by a train. Miraculously, the student survived, and later told police investigators that he'd been experimenting with how close he could get his head to a moving train without being hit.

2 Looking forward to an afternoon of sunbathing, Californian truck driver Larry Waters hooked 45 weather balloons to his deckchair, then tied the chair to his jeep. Waters drifted up to a height of 30ft and settled back to relax. However, he hadn't tied the rope very securely and, when the knot came loose, shot up to 16,000ft. After several hours of high altitude panic, Waters was finally rescued when he drifted across the approach corridor of Los Angeles International airport.

1 Ken E.Richardson's folly was two-fold. First of all, he accepted his cousin Derrick's invitation to play a game of Russian roulette near their home in Minneapolis. Then, seeing as neither Derrick nor Ken possessed a revolver, Ken kicked off the proceedings by loading a semi-automatic – a gun with only one firing chamber. Not surprisingly, Derrick emerged the victor.

12-31-95 6:21:26A

12-31-95 6:21:47A

...then puts it down to pick the pocket of a customer...

...loses it to the assistant...

21*48A

12-31-95 6*21*54A

...and finally has to run for it

This moronic robber (top) is pointing a gun at a shop assistant...

PORN

If the shame and cost of renting rude films from the video store is too much for you, why not simply make your own?

Lighting The set should be fairly well lit, or you'll see nothing. However, a darker studio could prove valuable in covering up beer guts and unsightly body hair. Your punters should be able to see what's going on without being put off by an unwarranted hairy arse or folds of cellulite.

Set It's much more convenient and realistic – "real" porn being the thing of the moment – if you set your skin-flick in your trusted bedroom. Not only will you be safe from prying eyes, but you'll also have the time to get the shots exactly right.

Technique It's always best to map out your actors' movements with the camera in mind – plus, you won't want anyone refusing to perform a "routine". Always remember that nervous fumblings do not a good porno make: you want slick transfers from one position to another.

The law The legality of filming a willing partner and yourself "at it" is vague, to say the least. With no actual law preventing the filming (as opposed to the reproduction and subsequent sale of the film or video), it seems that the only stumbling block depends on how many people are involved. Although two people can do as they wish behind closed doors, it become confused when a third person is present, because "private" then becomes "public". And you're sure to be in trouble if the police have any reason to search your property and, as a result, find a record of your carnal capers. So the bottom line is keep the numbers down and the copies to a minimum.

Bed The major player in the porn game is the bed. No headboard is needed and the footboard shouldn't obscure any low-to-the-mattress shots. A firm, hard bed, such as a futon, is best, as it doesn't make waves, which could put your studs off their game. And definitely no itchy woollen sheets.

ON A BUDGET

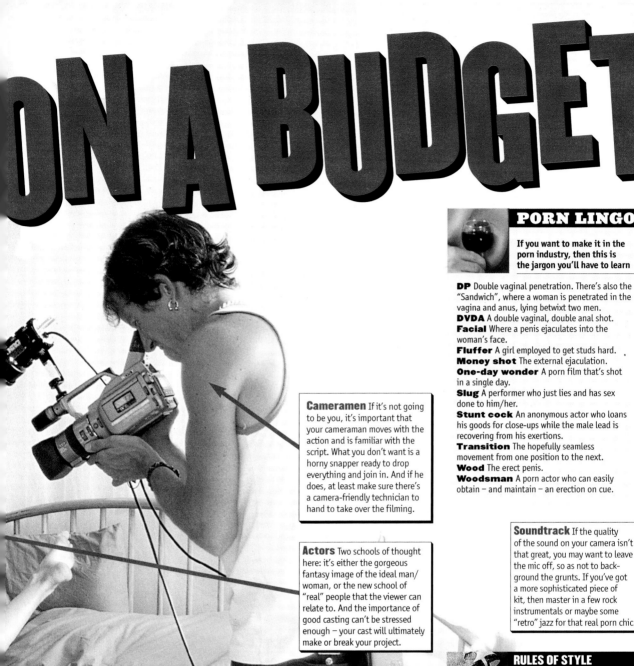

PORN LINGO

If you want to make it in the porn industry, then this is the jargon you'll have to learn

DP Double vaginal penetration. There's also the "Sandwich", where a woman is penetrated in the vagina and anus, lying betwixt two men.

DVDA A double vaginal, double anal shot.

Facial Where a penis ejaculates into the woman's face.

Fluffer A girl employed to get studs hard.

Money shot The external ejaculation.

One-day wonder A porn film that's shot in a single day.

Slug A performer who just lies and has sex done to him/her.

Stunt cock An anonymous actor who loans his goods for close-ups while the male lead is recovering from his exertions.

Transition The hopefully seamless movement from one position to the next.

Wood The erect penis.

Woodsman A porn actor who can easily obtain – and maintain – an erection on cue.

Cameramen If it's not going to be you, it's important that your cameraman moves with the action and is familiar with the script. What you don't want is a horny snapper ready to drop everything and join in. And if he does, at least make sure there's a camera-friendly technician to hand to take over the filming.

Actors Two schools of thought here: it's either the gorgeous fantasy image of the ideal man/woman, or the new school of "real" people that the viewer can relate to. And the importance of good casting can't be stressed enough – your cast will ultimately make or break your project.

Soundtrack If the quality of the sound on your camera isn't that great, you may want to leave the mic off, so as not to background the grunts. If you've got a more sophisticated piece of kit, then master in a few rock instrumentals or maybe some "retro" jazz for that real porn chic.

Outfits Nurses' outfits and leather may be alluring, but you'll need to see good close-ups of genitalia if your film's to succeed. And if you go with the fantasy uniforms, you may need to edit out wasted time accrued through tackling zippers and buttons. The best kit is that found on the floor.

RULES OF STYLE WITH DIGBY CRESCENT

Listen and learn as Digby wades through your queries...

Dear FHM,
I confided to a pal at Job Club that I could no longer get hard for my girl, and he said that he watched the odd hard-core flick to "spice" him up. So, boosted by his advice, I too started to browse through photos and magazines, which I kept hidden in a box. As he claimed, my manhood was revived – only now I find my own company more satisfying.

A man can make love to himself without any shame, but self-gratification should never outweigh the joy of two bodies entwined in mutual lust. Maybe you should introduce your lady to the photos and make her a part of the proceedings. Then you could progress to watching hard-core porn films together, and maybe taking in the occasional peep show.

Porn players' lounge

Pull up a bar-stool and meet the Larry Oliviers and Richard Burtons of the naked screen...

John's novelty wine dispenser never took off

JOHN HOLMES

Known as The King by fans and colleagues alike, Holmes packed a whopping 14in into his tight Seventies slacks. Holmes starred in some of the most famous porn flicks of his time – around 2,220 of them – and is considered by many to be the most versatile stud in the business. Unfortunately, he became a raging cocaine addict and descended into the shadowy scene of the LA underworld during the Eighties, eventually dying of AIDS in 1988.

JEFF STRYKER

The glamourpuss of modern-day porn, Stryker actually made less than 30 films. The pretty boy made his debut in 1986, starring in the gay porn flick *Bigger Than Life*, before moving on to *Powertool* and other classics. He subsequently gave up porn for modelling and promoting self-defence videos.

KING DONG

Nobody's sure if this man's behemoth of a cock was real or not. It's alleged his enormous 2ft dong was nothing but a prosthetic used as a clever marketing ploy by his manager to satisfy the stereotype of the well-hung black man. Some Seventies critics claimed they'd seen different actors masquerading as Dong in his numerous films and merchandise – the most popular spin-off being the King Dong Pack Of Cards.

Margold: chicken-lover

BILL MARGOLD

Big Bill is a true stalwart of the genre: ably assisted by his ten-inch terror, he can be found co-starring with Holmes in many Seventies porno classics. Nowadays, however, the ageing swordsman acts as the industry's chronicler and is a fervent campaigner for freedom of expression. He's also the man who shagged a cold chicken in *Intimate Lessons*.

RON JEREMY

Nicknamed "The Hedgehog", the former high-school teacher starred in over 1,000 flicks and was consulted on the set of *Boogie Nights*. Moved into the mainstream during the Eighties with a walk-on part in *The Chase* and played a bank teller in *Killing Zoe*. He also released a rap CD under the moniker of "Headboard". Jeremy can apparently suck his own dick, too.

Jeremy: cocksucker

How it all started

Hark back to yesteryear with the films that made it all possible...

These days, porn films are fairly lame, basically. Now that porno's been around for years, we're desensitised to the images, and there are only so many things a well-hung stud can do to a willing woman. But in the good old days, porn was actually considered ground-breaking – and shocking.

Deep Throat (1972) Woman can't orgasm through normal intercourse. But she finds out that she gets off on giving blokes blow-jobs.
Behind The Green Door (1972) The forerunner to the modern skin-flick, this had everything – anal, oral and the sandwich.
Babyface (1975) Lady tempts men by dressing up as a girl. Shaves thatch for finishing touch. One scene consists of a woman swinging in a hammock while being shagged senseless by a whole host of men.

GERARD DAMIANO'S
DEEP THROAT
HOW FAR DOES A GIRL HAVE TO GO TO UNTANGLE HER TINGLE?
EASTMANCOLOR Ⓧ ADULTS ONLY

MARILYN CHAMBERS
Behind the Green Door

So you really think you're in with a chance with your new girlfriend? But before you buy in a couple of extra rashers for Saturday breakfast, get her to put her mark on this little contract...

The FHM Pre-Shag Agreement

I, THE UNDERSIGNED, AGREE THAT

1 In the unlikely event of my not having an orgasm after you've drunkenly rolled on top of me and pumped away for five minutes, wheezing like an old man with emphysema, I shall politely fake one. And it'll be a really good act too, with me saying stuff like "So *this* is screwing!" and howling like a cat that's being repeatedly jabbed with a compass.

2 Should your mother show me any photos of you as a child, like those ones taken at your auntie's wedding where you've got a velvet bow-tie and a pudding-bowl haircut, I shall make no comment. Ever. Or even look at you in a way that suggests they are at all "funny".

3 I fully understand that a woman's main role in any relationship is to take the blame. So when you stub your toe in the bathroom or your football team lose, I agree that – by some complex scientific equation incomprehensible to women – it will be my fault. Even if I wasn't there.

4 Whenever my friends and I get together for a girlie chat, I will tell them that you are better hung than a large-balled Himalayan yak.

5 And I will also mention this to *your* friends. A lot.

6 After sex (which I shall *never* refer to as "making love"), I will not expect you to cuddle me for hours 'til your arm goes dead. Nor will I let my hair annoyingly get in your face.

7 I will never, ever give your penis a "cute" nickname.

8 In bed, I will be keen as mustard to try any novel sexual position you fancy. Especially ones where I do all the work and you just lie there, grinning.

9 I will ruthlessly interrogate my attractive female friends and inform you if any of them have the slightest bisexual tendencies. Then I'll invite them round for dinner. And hide their car keys so they have to stay.

10 After we split up, I will never sleep with any of your friends or colleagues. Or anyone else you have ever met. Or may one day meet. And if men attempt to chat me up, I will solemnly inform them that you have "ruined me for other men".

11 I understand that mechanical objects like cars, computer games and remote control devices are beyond the comprehension of women. I will only make a fool of myself if I attempt to operate them, so you're in charge of the lot. Except for the iron and the washing machine, of course.

Signed ....

Date ....

IT'S ALL POISON

We looked at a typical bloke's diet and found out that, sadly, if you are what you eat, then most men are walking, talking chemical plants

CHOCOLATE
Lovely chocolate, for so long seen as simply the indulgence of a sweet tooth, could also be wrecking the temple that is your body. Most chocolate bars contain lindane, a highly toxic pesticide which'll make more than your teeth rot.

BEER
Nothing wrong with a pint, you think, apart from the fact that it'll make you fat and act like a fool. You are so wrong, my friend. Beer-makers don't have to list the ingredients in their brews, which include enzymes, stabilisers and sulphites – all good for a throbbing headache. Sulphites, in fact, can cause potentially fatal asthma attacks.

HAMBURGERS
Where to start with the world's favourite fast food? The meat used in some burgers is the most unpleasant bits of a cow ground up and pumped full of water, flavouring and preservatives; take-away food, conveniently, doesn't have to list its ingredients by law; and by 1997, only half of the abattoirs in Britain met EC hygiene standards.

SPARE RIBS

Antibiotics are routinely fed to farmyard animals, which means that the bugs most dangerous to man are getting exposed to drugs further down the food chain – and becoming ever more resistant. Eighty-seven per cent of salmonella strains are now resistant to antibiotics. And barbecue sauce.

CHIPS

The potato is much maligned: it's a great source of vitamins, fibre and protein. Tragically, half of all potatoes tested in 1995 contained aldicarb – a highly toxic insecticide suspected of being able to cause cancer.

GOOD STUFF

It seems that if you want to avoid unhealthy food, you're reduced to a very basic diet of carrots and water. There is, however, a catch. You'll have to grow your vegetables yourself, because if they're pulled from the sod of a large agribusiness they are probably shot through with pesticides. Maybe it's the chemicals which keep bugs off the plants that allows carrots to help you see in the dark.

PORK PIE

There is nothing quite like a good pork pie. Delicious. And full of nitrates, saturated fat and reconstituted animal products. Enjoy – and picture your blood pressure rocketing.

TAKE-AWAY CURRY

Contaminated cooked meat products can be lethal. A strain of *E. coli* bacteria caused 19 deaths and over 400 serious illnesses in one horrific outbreak in Scotland in 1997. Rare until ten years ago, the pernicious bug is now rife.

FLAVOURED INSTANT PUDDINGS

Just add milk – the only natural thing you'll get out of these pools of rancid chemical filth. Emulsifiers, gelling agents, sodium pyrophosphates, colourings, sweeteners and lindane – a pesticide. After a few of these you'll be setting off Geiger counters. Evil.

CRISPS

The world's number-one snack food is chock full of life-threatening ingredients. That's right, they're not just potatoes, but also saturated fat (excellent for clogged arteries) and artificial flavourings too complex to analyse.

RULES OF STYLE WITH DIGBY CRESCENT

Listen and learn as Digby wades through your queries...

Dear FHM,

I have been lucky enough to meet a truly gorgeous girl. She has invited me down to her father's yacht – needless to say they are very wealthy. My problem is this: I know we will be eating seafood, but I haven't got a clue how to eat crab, lobster or unshelled prawn. Can you instruct?

Ah, seafood. Always tricky to the beginner. The big deal with crustaceans is to extract the juicy bits from the animal's ever-protective shell. Lobster and crab are both likely to come opened and cleaned; however, the prawn will generally appear in full armour. Whip the head off, take the legs and peel them and the accompanying shell away from the body, and pop the flesh out. If you really want to extend your appreciation, suck the pungent juice from the leftover heads.

IS SHE A SLUT?

Did your parents wince when your girl first went round for dinner? Has your best mate started avoiding you? Sweet Lord, you could be seeing a slapper...

1 The milkman clinks his bottles and says "good morning". What does she do?
a) Scuttles back indoors, mortified that he's seen her in a nightie.
b) Winks at him and says, "It could be even better..."
c) Wishes him good morning back and has a chat about the problems of parking a milkfloat.

2 When discussing sexual exploits with her friends, what does she do?
a) Simply refuses to join in.
b) Crooks her little finger, wiggles it up and down and roars, "It made a chipolata look like Nelson's Column, eh girls?"
c) Makes glancing references to a couple of occasions, without getting too detailed.

3 You're watching The Girlie Show. What does she do?
a) Begs you to turn this rubbish off. Feminism doesn't mean girls behaving like blokes.
b) Shrieks and yells abuse at any male who crosses the screen.
c) Starts off ignoring it, then gradually becomes drawn in.

4 What would she say if you mooted a new sex position?
a) "I'd rather not. Two is plenty."
b) "I haven't done that since I was underneath Brighton Pier in '92 with a bottle of Woodpecker and Jason Beasley!"
c) "Go on then, I'll give it a try."

5 Who do her two closest friends resemble?
a) Charlotte and Emily Bronte.
b) The Fat Slags in *Viz*.
c) The giggling receptionists in *I'm Alan Partridge*.

6 Has she ever:
■ Stripped a Corsican waiter.
■ Given a blow-job to a man whose name she doesn't know.
■ Thrown up 19 rum and blacks in a taxi.
■ Said: "Ooh, that Doctor Ross, he makes me right horny."
■ Broken a stiletto heel and gone on to the club anyway, listing like a ship in a storm.
■ Said: "That Pauline Calf might be a tart, but she's got her head screwed on."
■ Streaked her hair using a home peroxide kit and a swimming cap.
■ Bought an ankle chain through mail-order.
■ Had a snogging contest to see how many tongues she could get in a night.
■ Had a catfight with another woman in a pub toilet.
■ Been thrown off a late bus.
■ Danced with 12 drunken mates to the *Macarena*, then begged the DJ to put it on again.

7 What was her first sexual experience?
a) A mutually trusting, pre-planned session in his parents' bed – with their blessing.
b) A romp down the park with seven of the Catford Posse and a bottle of Thunderbird for afters.
c) Forgettable, and slightly depressing.

8 To seduce her, what would you sing in her ear?
a) "Daa de da de dadadada daa" – Rachmaninov's third piano concerto.
b) "Wo-ohohoh-ooh, myster-ious girl, I wanna get close to you..."
c) "And after all, you're my wonderwalll!... lalalala laaaa..."

9 Who is her role model?
a) Mo Mowlam.
b) Melinda Messenger.
c) Meg Matthews.

10 How did she learn her blow-job technique?
a) From *The Joy Of Sex*.
b) Down a friend's dad's shed.
c) From her first proper boyfriend.

11 When did she first reveal her body to you?
a) After some gentle encouragement, with the lights off.
b) When she spotted you, a stranger, and lifted up her crop top, shouting: "Get a load of these, smiler!"
c) The first time she got reasonably drunk.

12 Pick out the presents your girlfriend would buy you from this list:
■ Fluffy gonk.
■ *Songs For Lovers*, Volume 16.
■ Humourous apron with a pair of comedy breasts on it.
■ Posing pouch.
■ Gold-plated St Christopher.
■ Mug which reveals a naked woman when it heats up.
■ Pina colada-flavoured condoms.
■ Bottle of Midori melon liqueur.

13 What's her attitude to infidelity?
a) She couldn't take the betrayal of trust – it would be over.
b) She'd "rip your balls off and stuff them in your fat gob".
c) She'd cry a lot.

14 It's a school reunion. How does she greet her old chums?
a) "Monica and Caroline! How's the families?"
b) "Raaaaay! Chantelle and Tina! Getting any these days?"
c) "Anna! Sue! You've lost weight!"

15 Tick the destinations she'd like to visit:
■ Ibiza
■ Blackpool
■ Newquay
■ Southend
■ Benidorm
■ Kos
■ Bondi beach
■ Marbella
■ Hawaii
■ Disneyworld

16 How does she describe St Moritz cigarettes?
a) "Those appalling menthols."
b) "Saint dead sophisticated."
c) "San Moritz."

17 Does she fancy any Liverpool footballers?
Yes/No

18 Has she ever chanted anything in a public place?
Yes/No

19 Tick the body parts she leaves uncovered on a big night out:
■ Neck
■ Cleavage
■ Thighs
■ Stomach
■ Shoulders
■ Nipples

20 Which of these older men would she prefer to go on a date with?
a) Alaistair Burnett.
b) Peter Stringfellow.
c) Mick Jagger.

21 What does she like to read in bed?
a) Jane Austen; Virago Modern Classics; Sylvia Plath poetry.
b) Woman's Realm cartoon books called *My Doctor, My Love*; Black Lace erotica; the instructions on a packet of condoms.
c) Last month's *Marie Claire*; Martin Amis; Jilly Cooper.

Rita's jitterbugging kept the boys occupied as Pearl Harbor burned

22 Which of these would she use as a masturbatory aid?

- [ ] *Fiesta*'s One For The Ladies
- [ ] A Jessica Rabbit vibrator
- [ ] Japanese love-balls
- [ ] Mazola
- [ ] A vibrating egg
- [ ] A Mars bar
- [ ] An Asti Spumante bottle

23 What did she used to do with her dolls?

a) Line them up and pretend to teach them history.
b) Splutter with laughter while she made them have sex.
c) Chop their hair off, colour their faces in, lose their clothes.

24 In her teens, if her brother's friends came round, what did she do?

a) Stayed in her room discussing ponies with her best friend.
b) Offered to let them touch her up for a sherbet fountain and a can of dandelion and burdock.

c) Ignored them while they played their Emerson Lake and Palmer LPs and smoked cannabis.

25 Are her legs Persil-white and covered in blue veins?
Yes/No

26 Would some slight chubbiness be no impediment to her sporting a micro-mini?
Yes/No

27 Has she ever worn her hair in crispily-gelled ringlets under a neon yellow towelling band?
Yes/No

28 Does she own greying Puma trainers, white patent platform boots and plastic stilettos?
Yes/No

29 Buying under-wear with seduction in mind, where would she go?
a) Marks and Spencer or BHS.
b) Anne Summers or the small ads in the *Sunday Sport*.
c) La Perla or Agent Provocateur.

"Well, as long as it's done tasteful."

30 If she had a baby, what would she call it?
a) Toby or Sophie.
b) Elvis or Toyah.
c) Jack or Emma.

31 What's her favourite drug?
a) Aspirin, Feminax.
b) Wizz, jellies.
c) Cannabis, and the odd hallucinogen in her youth.

32 She's drunk, with you and your mates. Which of these would she do?
■ Challenge them all to a drinking contest.
■ Strip them, roaring: "What's that, a bleedin' thimble?"
■ Drag them to Stagz 'N' Henz so they can all do The Time-warp.
■ Shag each of them on the snooker table round the back.

33 You're at a wedding. What does she say?
a) "Us next, darling, hmm?"
b) "Bloody hell, that usher's a bit of alright – he's what, 15? Still, never too young to learn!"
c) "I hope there's enough to drink later."

34 Which of these would she say to indicate her need for a toilet?
a) "Could you tell me where the ladies' loo is, please?"
b) "Fuckin' 'ell, I'm going to wazz meself in a minute."
c) "Where's the toilet?"

35 What's her ideal job?
a) Presenting *Newsnight*.
b) Oiling the Chippendales.
c) Something fun, glamorous and well-paid.

36 What does she do in her lunch-break?
a) Goes to the gym for a work-out.
b) Paints her nails scarlet; reads her horoscope in *My Guy*; apply fake tan.
c) Meets friends for lunch.

37 How did she get her current job?
a) By getting good qualifications and showing boundless energy.
b) By sleeping with the man who interviewed her.
c) Through the friend of a friend.

38 Would she be unfaithful to you?
a) Only if her life depended on it.
b) Only if the guy was breathing.
c) Only if your relationship had irretrievably broken down.

39 Which of these films would she like to see?
■ *Steel Magnolias; Fame!*
■ *Felix The Cat; Emmanuelle.*
■ *Dirty Dancing; The Full Monty.*

40 You're taking her for a romantic meal. Where would she like to go?
a) Le Manoir aux Quatre Saisons.
b) A Harvester for all-you-can-eat Steak 'n' Strawberries.
c) The local Italian.

41 Under what circumstances would she strip on a bar?
a) In the midst of a nightmare.
b) Last summer, with her mate Kelly on an 18-30 to Ibiza.
c) Perhaps in her wildest sexual fantasies.

42 She says she's having "a quick drink after work". What does this entail?
a) A glass of chardonnay with a couple of colleagues.
b) Seventeen Malibu and cokes and five different Happy Hours.
c) A bottle of wine and a good giggle for two hours.

43 For your first kiss, what did she do?
a) Tilted her face, flower-like, until you sought her lips.
b) Shoved your hand inside her bra, saying, "Do I have to do everything myself?"
c) Tentatively brushed her mouth against yours?

44 You come too quickly. What does she say?
a) "Well, it gets it over with..."
b) "What was that, Trigger?"
c) "Never mind. Let's cuddle."

45 Would she cry over any of these things?
■ A picture of kittens.
■ The Queen Mother dying.
■ *Lady In Red*.
■ A Hallmark poem.
■ A character getting killed by a hit and run driver in *Neighbours*.

46 You secretly sent her photo to Readers' Wives. She is voted Wife Of The Month. Is she proud?
Yes/No

47 A male stripper asks her to feel down his G-string with her tongue for a banana. Does she comply?
Yes/No

48 She is on a coach. A group starts singing Blue Moon. What does she do?
a) Think what a romantic song it is.
b) Turns round, lowers her knickers and presses her bare bottom against the window.
c) Ignores them, assuming it's some football thing.

49 Where has she been happiest?
a) Touring the cathedrals of Italy after university.
b) Down the pavilion at the local park after school.
c) Inside a Donna Karan store after she got promoted.

50 What would she have on a car sticker?
a) "Martinmere Wildlife Trust".
b) "Don't come a-knockin' if this van's a-rockin'".
c) She wouldn't have a car sticker.

SCORING

■ Two ticks or more on list questions equal "b"; one tick equals "c"; no ticks equals "a".
■ Yes/No questions – score an extra "b" for all "yes" answers.
MOSTLY A Your girlfriend is the complete opposite of a slapper. To her, sex is a sacred act of trust and affection – she'll never visit a strip show, chant "down in one" at a posse of squaddies she's just met, or shout "I've 'ad 'im" at passers-by. You've been spared. But you also might be bored, as "outrageous" becomes a word you only use for the New World Selection prices at Oddbins.
MOSTLY B Your woman makes Lily Savage look like Joan Bakewell – a model of discretion and restraint. She's an out-and-out slag, born with a plastic cocktail stirrer in her mouth, whose only foreign phrase is "Si". She has 15 best mates, who she loves more than any man. She fancies you, but you talk too much – she prefers a man who speaks with his body. She's yours until her next Spanish holiday, when she'll be unfaithful 14 nights in a row with 27 different men.
MOSTLY C You have a woman so normal she's remarkable. A healthy attitude to sex coupled with a realistic appraisal of life's priorities typifies her, and while you could never call her a slapper, she's certainly not boring. Slapperdom, however, is quite attractive – there's something dangerously appealing about that crass female energy which every girl secretly envies. Should you start getting too possessive, too dull or just too mature, there's every chance she'll opt to explore a new way of life, one where she'll loudly discusses your sexual failings with her mates in the pub and doesn't come home 'til three because she's been down an alley with an Italian waiter.

"My teeth are shocking" If your choppers resemble a set of leaning tombstones, don't leer with your mouth clamped shut like some hillbilly grandad – go to the dentist for a professional cleaning job. However, if your grin is simply a bit lopsided, leave well alone or you could weaken your teeth and end up with your molars in a glass by the age of 40.

"I've got dark rings under my eyes" If you've recently adopted the lifestyle of a top politician or international DJ, it's hardly surprising you're not looking bushy-tailed. But if you've been snoozing the hours away and still look like Alice Cooper, better check your diet – too much junk

many people mistake you for a welcome mat – or get waxed. The process takes 15 minutes of teeth-gritting, wax-strip ripping. Then it'll be six weeks before you start looking like The Fly again.

"I've got a stupid tattoo" Removing it won't be a breeze: laser treatment is very expensive but does the best job, surgical removal often leaves some scarring, and both will cost you. And if you've got a galleon in full sail across your back, God help you – and your wallet.

"My skin isn't kitten-soft anymore" If your skin is dry, scaly or flaky, you can try several things: work up a busking act as the Singing Detective, or shower

"I've got a shaving rash" If you've got skin like a new-born mink, it'll react badly to a blade. Minimise the agony by using a clean razor, a shaving brush and soap. Alternatively, try a shaving gel for sensitive complexions and pull your skin taut as you shave.

"I've got dandruff" If only half your scalp is suffering, you're an amnesiac actor from a shampoo ad. If it's all of it, then it should be cleared up by an anti-dandruff shampoo. And if the snow's still on your shoulders, it may not be dandruff at all, but a problem such as sebhorric eczema. See your GP for a big, proper lotion.

"My hair is ludicrous" Frizzy hair gets worse after harsh brushing, and even panics at damp air. Unless you shave it off,

you'll have to live with your Bonnie Langford explosion of curls, so use Frizz-Ease hair serum from John Frieda or a similar follicle-smoothing product. It's your only hope.

"My feet stink" Wash your feet twice a day and change your socks whenever they get fetid – every hour if need be. Use Scholl's deodorant foot spray, and always wear cotton socks and leather shoes – trainers are the sworn enemy of fragrance.

"I'm a freckleface" True gingers have skin like milk, burn in sunlight and are a riot of freckles come summer. So protect that epidermis with an SPF25 tanning lotion, and wear a hat, shades and T-shirt at all times. Or look like a lobster and endure the laughter.

You may not be God's gift, but for pity's sake, man – make the best of yourself

SMARTEN UP!

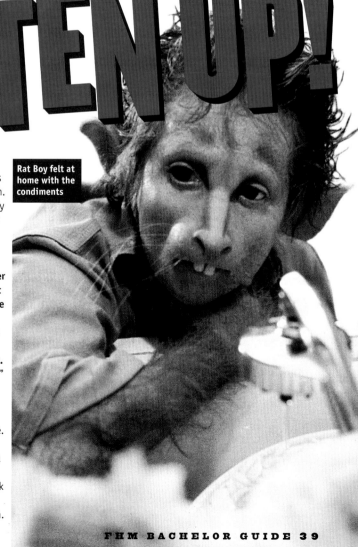

Rat Boy felt at home with the condiments

food, alcohol and drugs can suck youthful vitality from your face.

"My breath stinks" No woman wants to stick her tongue into the oral equivalent of the Batcave. Follow these basic rules: brush your teeth at least twice a day; floss regularly; swill with mouthwash every day. If that doesn't do it, you may have some hateful adenoidal or abdominal complaint. See a doctor at once, and don't kiss anyone in the meantime.

"My eyebrows meet" Women never trust a man whose eyebrows meet in the middle – so you'll have to pluck them. Use tweezers with a slanted edge, pressing a damp cloth on first to loosen the hairs, and tweeze one hair at a time. Don't, whatever you do, go too far, or you'll look permanently surprised. And ridiculous.

"I've got a hairy back" You can always lie naked in front of the door at parties and count how

rather than bathe to rinse away dead skin. Avoid perfumed soaps and gels in favour of an E45 wash. You could also exfoliate with body scrub and seal moisture in using a light body lotion.

"I'm bald" And there's nothing you can do about it. It's genetic. Keep what you've got short, rather than sport a selection of pathetic wisps, and if you're really desperate you could try Regain TM from the chemist – £30 for 60ml, plus no guarantees and a sniggering assistant. Best live with it, Kojak.

"I've got loads of blackheads" Okay – steam your face over a bowl of hot water, then wrap a tissue round your fingers and press the skin around the blackie. It should pop out; but if not, gouging it with a nail will leave a livid bruise, so don't. Body Shop do blackhead squeezers. They look instruments of torture, but work – if you can be arsed to use them.

KOBAL

There's bound to be a time in your life when you feel you simply aren't a man without a bit of facial hair. You obviously can't grow an instant moustache – unless you're Italian, of course – so why not pop on one of these *FHM* favourites?

FACE FUNGUS!

THE SAR'NT-MAJOR
Perfectly trimmed, waxed into fine points and capable of extension to ludicrous lengths. Military men, if they are going to experiment with facial hair, have to keep it immaculate.

THE CHIN-WARMER
The history of this stray piece of hair hanging just under the mouth is vague: apparently southern Californian beach bums were the first people to start growing them in the late Seventies "for something to do". Now only seen on surfers and Tom Waites. Preposterous.

THE GAY BUSH
True, you don't have to be gay to sport this fine face-hair – look at David Seaman – but Freddie Mercury *et al* are the driving force behind the clone's favourite. It should, ideally, droop over the lip and get milk and food in it.

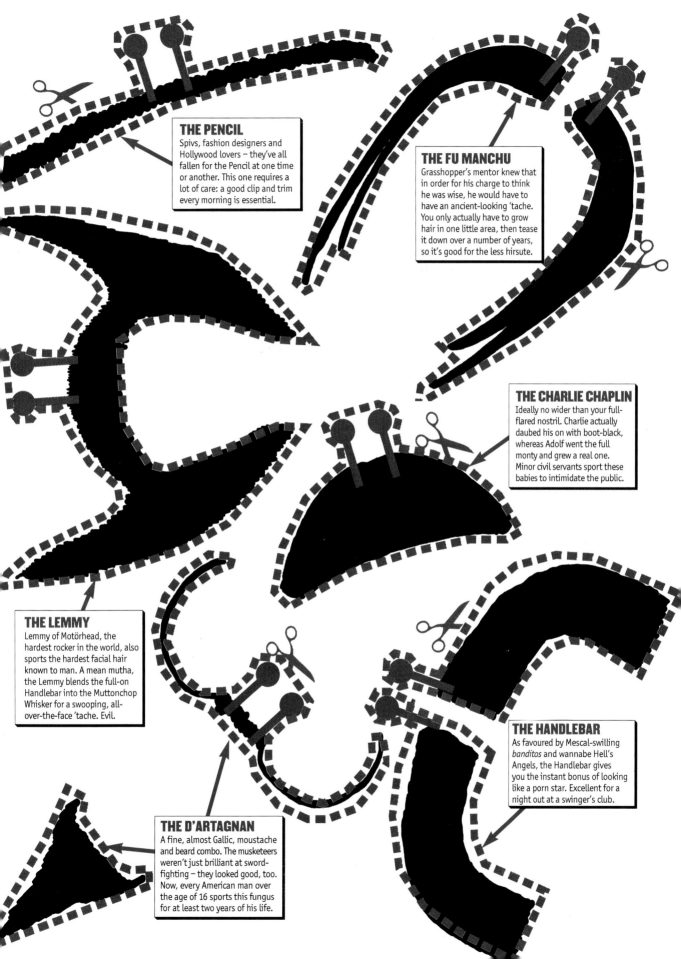

THE PENCIL

Spivs, fashion designers and Hollywood lovers – they've all fallen for the Pencil at one time or another. This one requires a lot of care: a good clip and trim every morning is essential.

THE FU MANCHU

Grasshopper's mentor knew that in order for his charge to think he was wise, he would have to have an ancient-looking 'tache. You only actually have to grow hair in one little area, then tease it down over a number of years, so it's good for the less hirsute.

THE CHARLIE CHAPLIN

Ideally no wider than your full-flared nostril. Charlie actually daubed his on with boot-black, whereas Adolf went the full monty and grew a real one. Minor civil servants sport these babies to intimidate the public.

THE LEMMY

Lemmy of Motörhead, the hardest rocker in the world, also sports the hardest facial hair known to man. A mean mutha, the Lemmy blends the full-on Handlebar into the Muttonchop Whisker for a swooping, all-over-the-face 'tache. Evil.

THE HANDLEBAR

As favoured by Mescal-swilling *banditos* and wannabe Hell's Angels, the Handlebar gives you the instant bonus of looking like a porn star. Excellent for a night out at a swinger's club.

THE D'ARTAGNAN

A fine, almost Gallic, moustache and beard combo. The musketeers weren't just brilliant at sword-fighting – they looked good, too. Now, every American man over the age of 16 sports this fungus for at least two years of his life.

THE BREASTS To male eyes, there is nothing complex about a woman's breasts – two lumps on the front of the chest that account for a relatively small portion of the female body. In a woman, however, there is a direct link between the breasts and the brain – a link that, unfortunately, is regularly disrupted or faulty. The two messages sent along the line of communication are "my breasts are too small" and "my breasts are too big". These electronic impulses bear no relation to the actual size of the glands.

THE INDEX FINGER Women have a special finger, which has a "sponge fibre" at the knuckle joint. Men don't need this safety feature, because the pressure put on their joints in a lifetime is minimal. Women, however, suffer from Repetitive Dial Strain, and need this unique adaptation to avoid cramping in later life.

THE BUTTOCKS Most of the female buttock is, in fact, designed for utilitarian rather than sexual use. While it is true that the buttock can be used as a device to lure men, its primary purpose is to serve as a padded, moulded cushion. This enables a woman to sit snugly for hour after hour after hour without the discomfort of sores. Believed to have co-evolved alongside the "sponge fibre" joint (see above).

THE BRAIN The male brain has three main parts: the cerebellum, the brainstem and the forebrain. Women, however, only have two sections. One, the trivialevum, takes up 87% of the brain and is filled with information men don't need to store: stuff like how many calories are in a double fudge cake, birthdays of people they hardly know, and the names of flowers. The other 13% is reserved for telephone numbers, with a small section for unfounded neurosis.

THE SHOULDER Not much to a shoulder, you'd think, beyond knocking into doors and hanging a jacket from. Not so! A woman's hormonally-adjusted shoulder has a unique swivel disk which automatically rolls the shoulder across the body in a defensive motion should the female detect a slight from any living being. This "snubbing" is completely imagined in 75% of cases.

THE DIGESTIVE SYSTEM The male digestive system can handle all sorts of stuff: cheese from a tube, raw beef, wool. The female system is more delicate: it has a massive reservoir reserved for chocolate, and another, much smaller tract to deal with tiny salads and mineral water. Uniquely, women can swap between the two systems. Sometimes in a single meal sitting.

THE ABDOMEN Within this section of the woman, two essential elements are stored. One is the Biological Clock, which starts ticking around the time a woman realises that work is a pain in the arse. The other is a tiny nodule adjacent to the clock where the famous "female instinct" is stored. This nodule is vestigial, and consequently remains unused during a woman's lifetime.

WHAT'S IN A WOMAN?

The human body is made up of, like, water and stuff. And some teeth. This, however, only applies to the male; the female, beautiful thing that she is, has contents unique to herself. Exactly what is it that fills out a lady?

PHOTOGRAPHY: ADAM LAWRENCE

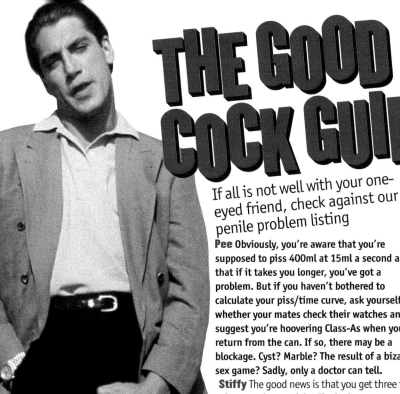

THE GOOD COCK GUIDE

If all is not well with your one-eyed friend, check against our penile problem listing

Pee Obviously, you're aware that you're supposed to piss 400ml at 15ml a second and that if it takes you longer, you've got a problem. But if you haven't bothered to calculate your piss/time curve, ask yourself whether your mates check their watches and suggest you're hoovering Class-As when you return from the can. If so, there may be a blockage. Cyst? Marble? The result of a bizarre sex game? Sadly, only a doctor can tell.

Stiffy The good news is that you get three to four erections a night. The bad news: most of them are seamlessly worked into dreams about giant turnips. If you find yourself apparently impotent, if you can muster one "night" erection of longer than five minutes and with a rigidity of over 60 per cent, you're okay.

Blood There's about 100ml of blood in the average erection. And it needs a decent supply of healthy, oxygenated blood. Tiredness, illness, and standing on your head can all hinder performance. Conversely, having an erection for more than four hours makes you less of a stud, more of a man in grave danger. Instead of waving it at your girlfriend, shouting, "Come on down, there's plenty for everyone," you should decamp to your nearest A&E.

Spots The penis is a warm home for many nasties, such as herpes, warts, boils and fungal infections. Herpes is recognisable from its sporadic blister outbreaks, flu-like symptoms and cackling ex-girlfriends; warts are cauliflower-like eruptions; and boils are red, angry lumps with a yellow head. Fungal infections are recognisable by flaky, dry skin. For every last one, the doctor beckons.

Ejaculating In your teens, you do it at least once a night, generally into your mum's freshly laundered sheets. In your twenties, it's every other night, and at least occasionally into a girlfriend. But it's downhill from there. And if you're keen on parenthood, don't ejaculate too often or the sperm won't have time to regenerate. If ejaculation halts altogether, discounting tantric sex, you'll have to see a pro. That's a doctor, not a prostitute...

Latinos: cock-obsessed

HOW TO DO A GOOD JOB INTERVIEW
You're hired!

Why are job interviews so terrifying to the majority of us? Well, your future is on the line, you don't want to look like a gimp, and the man sitting opposite you holds all the cards. So the very least you can do is make yourself look and sound good.

■ **Practice** Apply for lots of jobs, even those you aren't so interested in. You will pick up interview tricks and technique, and learn what to expect.

■ **Make sure that you stay calm** Don't rub your nose, cover your mouth, dart your eyes around or laugh nervously: if you appear tense then the interviewer will become tense, too. You'll also look as though you have something to hide.

■ **Research** Make sure that you know the company and the work it does and be sure you really want to work for them. Ask for a company brochure before the interview, and bloody well read it.

■ **Prepare answers** You should have a selection of confident-sounding answers for standard questions such as: "Why do you want this job?" and "What can you offer us?" If you ask yourself a question at home and can't think of an answer, it is unlikely one will spring to mind in the interview.

■ **Don't be intimidated** Your interviewer is only another human being, so talk to him or her as you would someone you know well and respect. If you're intimidated, they'll think you lack backbone.

■ **Dress well and make a good impression** They will want to see how you would dress for that job, so don't attempt to show character by dressing in cargo pants and a Dead Kennedys T-shirt.

■ **Be civil** Shake hands when introduced. Say please and thank you when offered something. Don't sit down until someone asks you. You may not like this fawning, but if you get the job you can soon revert to your normal, belligerent self.

LIFE IMPROVING TIPS

In later years, Haystacks would thank his dad for his tough love

AM

Liberace distracted the puppies while the hessian sack was readied

I GAY?

If you've ever toyed with the idea of chewing the pillow, answer these questions and find out just how likely it is you're batting for the other side...

During puberty, most men come to a pretty definite decision about their sexuality. But since you passed that hurdle, have you considered the possibility that you might be wired for both gas and electric? To help you discover any suppressed urges hidden in your subconscious, *FHM* has designed the following questionnaire to tell you, once and for all – are you gay?

1 Your new flat-mate moves in. He is good-looking and well groomed. What do you do?

a) Ignore him. You won't have a chance with women if he's constantly hanging around, showing off his chiselled features.
b) Try to be friendly. Just because he looks like a million dollars doesn't mean he's a wanker.
c) Hang around outside the bathroom in the morning, hoping to get a peek of him in his boxers.

2 Which of these best describes your penis?

a) A girl-satisfying truncheon of pleasure.
b) Small and ugly. Although, when you catch a glimpse of it in the mirror, it seems quite cute.
b) Lonely.

3 Give yourself a point if you own a record by any of these artistes:

Take That, Abba, The Pet Shop Boys, Shirley Bassey, Gloria Gaynor, Kylie Minogue, Kavanagh, Barbra Streisand, Marc Almond, Judy Garland, Gina G, Dusty Springfield, Aqua, kd lang.

And take away a point if you own records by any of these artistes:

Cast, Happy Mondays, Baddiel & Skinner, Prodigy, Barry White, Iron Maiden, Paul Weller, Dodgy, The Clash, Shabba Ranks.

4 You decide to join the local gym. Why?

a) That's where the women with the best bodies hang out.
b) To improve your fitness levels.
c) There's no point wearing that white Dolce and Gabbana singlet unless you've got a six-pack nestling underneath.

5 Which of these statements best describes your attitude to Les Dennis?

a) "Never in televisual history has a less talented man managed to squirm his way onto the Saturday night schedule."
b) "Alright, his sketch show was shit, but you've got to admit that *Family Fortunes* is a classic gameshow format."
c) "A master of comic timing. And have you noticed the way he does a dinky pirouette back to the board when someone gives a stupid answer?"

6 It's a hot summer's night abroad, and you decide to hit the town in a pair of shorts. What is the ideal footwear combo?

a) A pair of Adidas Sambas.
b) A pair of sandals.
c) A fuck-off pair of 18-hole Dr Marten boots with steel toe-caps (and hiking socks underneath).

7 You're hooking up with a close female friend for the evening. What are your thoughts?

a) Yeah, she's a good mate, and we've known each other a long time. But if we get pissed enough, I wonder if I'll get further than that "just friends" snog we had last Christmas...
b) To sleep with her would destroy our friendship.
c) I hope she'll bring that ex of hers of hers along. The one who had a bit of a crisis and wound up before the judge on a cottaging charge.

Pink slippers: summerwear for clones

RULES OF STYLE WITH DIGBY CRESCENT

Listen and learn as Digby wades through your queries...

Dear FHM,
Although I consider myself to be hetero to the core, just recently I've been drawn to certain things which, I think, might mean I'm turning gay. I have stopped buying pop records and now enjoy the soundtracks of classic musicals; I buy flowers for my desk each morning; and I'm wearing purple more often than not. How can I tell whether or not I am truly gay?

My dear mixed-up friend, liking a spot of Liza Minnelli and sticking a vase of pansies on your desk doesn't make a man a mincer. There are, in fact, much clearer pointers to one's sexuality: Do you get wood watching Magnum PI? Do you check out guys' buns with lust, rather than simple jealousy? Either way, go with the flow. Wearing purple is bad, though.

Cocktails: you might as well be wearing a sign

8 **What are your views on the moustache?**
a) It's something middle-aged men grow to draw attention away from the fact that they're going bald.
b) It's distinctive on the right bloke.
c) It's the ultimate in butch – nothing beats a bushy handlebar!

9 **A leather-clad traffic cop pulls you over on the hard shoulder of the motorway. What is your reaction?**
a) "I was only doing 95…"
b) Get ready with the smiles – I'll get away with it if I can turn on the charm.
c) Oh, dear, I'm speeding. I suppose he'll have to be *very* firm with me.

10 **You're taking a piss in a public toilet when George Michael walks in, drops his pants and suggests you take a look at the nicotine patch on his buttocks. What do you say?**
a) "Hello? Hello? Is that the LAPD? He's at it again, I'm afraid."
b) "Uh, okay. So you reckon that works better than inhalers?"
c) "Very nice from the back, darling, but goatees just don't do it for me. I don't suppose you've got Andrew Ridgeley's number on you?"

11 **Give yourself a point if you own any of the following items:**
One of those toilet rolls with a doll in a dress stuck through the middle; a bottle of poppers; pink, fluffy slippers; a bottle of Campari and one of lemonade.

12 **Who did you have your first crush on?**
a) Samantha Fox.
b) Sarah Greene.
c) The Six Million Dollar Man.

13 **EastEnders is on TV, but you have to work late. Do you…**
a) Not give a shit. You haven't watched it since you were 16.
b) Shrug your shoulders and

Poppers: get a real man's drug habit

catch the omnibus on Sunday.
c) Resign. Any job that comes in the way of Grant Mitchell is a job not worth having.

14 **Your mother says she's coming to stay for the weekend. What do you think?**
a) Grin and bear it. Just hope the old bat goes to bed early so you can nip down the pub.
b) Fine. You haven't seen her in ages – it's time you repaid her for bringing you into the world.
c) It's wonderful news! She's a beautiful, strong woman and you'll be able to take her shopping for clothes.

15 **Some friends you haven't seen for ages ring up to say they're paying a surprise visit. How do you cater for them?**
a) Get ready to traipse down the chip shop.
b) Raid the kitchen cupboard and knock up a nice pasta sauce.
c) Prepare an elaborate finger buffet incorporating Twiglets, cheese fondue, sponge fingers and jelly, carefully arranged with doilies for each guest.

The results

■ Give yourself one point for every "B" and three points for every "C". No points for "A".

Three points or below: There's no doubting your sexuality, is there? You're an irrepressible lady-killer, supremely skilled in the ways and wiles of women. In fact, you're so straight you might as well have a gold medallion surgically implanted onto your chest. Why is it, then, that so many women are able to resist your advances? Why is it, in fact, that they seem to go for the sort of blokes you secretly suspect are poncey switch-hitters feeling each other up in the cubicles. You'd never think of doing that, would you? Oh no.

Four to 18 points: There was a moment, aged 14, when you woke up with a raging hard-on after dreaming about Philip Scofield, but you put it down to coincidence. And you like women. Probably a lot. You're hetero, but strand you on a desert island with nobody for company but a group of gay men and the truth is you might crack.

Nineteen points or more: You're a homosexual. But you didn't really need us to tell you that. Either you already sleep with men, or you're one of those sad blokes who try to date women and claim their lack of interest in taking them to bed is due to "low sex drive". If that's the case, wise up and book your holiday in 'Frisco this year. You'll have a very good time, we promise.

I THINK
I'M COMING
OUT

Telling your parents that you're a full-on trouser traitor can be a difficult thing to do. So let them gently in on the secret with these handy cut-out-and-keep rosettes

I'M GLAD
TO BE
GAY!

JA Henckels five-piece knife set, cutting board and drawer

JA Henckels have been making top-notch knives since the 18th century – so they must know what they're doing by now. And by keeping them in their beech drawer, you can stop your best blades getting mixed up with the less expensive cutlery.
STOCKISTS 01428 658888

KITCHEN KIT

Ten gizmos to turn your kitchen into the best-equipped room in the house

Francis Francis espresso machine

Pricey, perhaps, at around £330, but failing to splash out on an espresso-maker for the kitchen is like saying that you can't be bothered to buy a sofa for the living room.
STOCKISTS 0171-349 8411

Tefal electric wok

Superb for when flatmates are hogging your kitchen's hob space, this state-of-the-art wok is the perfect aid to stir-frying. And it's got a variable thermo-stat, so you can even use it to keep dishes warm at the table, which will give you an excuse to show it off to everyone you're cooking for.
STOCKISTS 01604 762726

Barbecook stainless steel barbecue

With no need for firelighters, starter fluids and so on, this stand-alone barbecue is simple – but brilliant. You'll be wanting to take it outside during the summer, but the Italians who designed the thing also made it look stylish enough to stand proudly in the kitchen during the colder winter months.
STOCKISTS 0171-935 0689

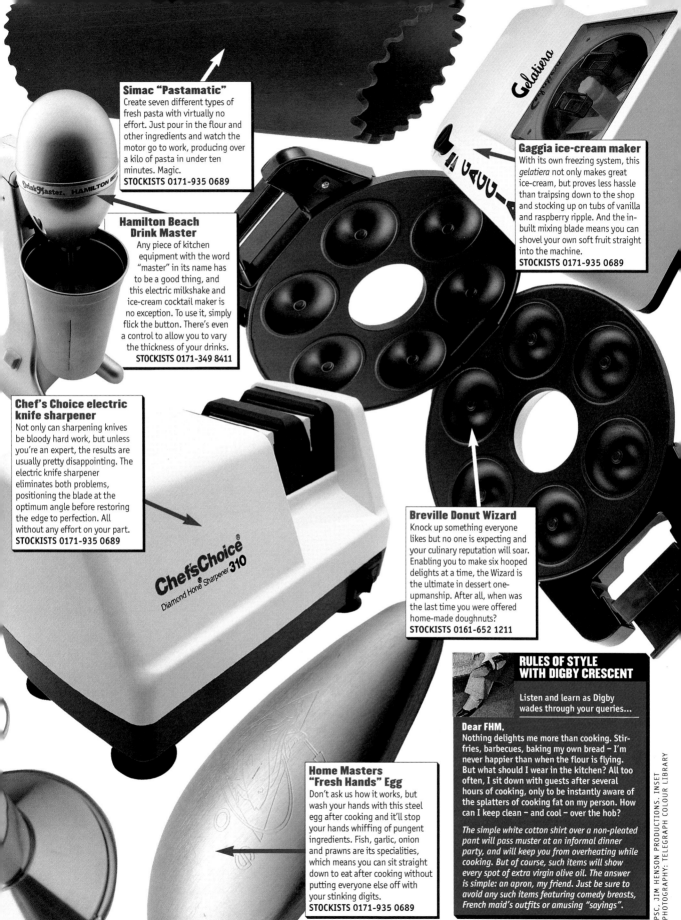

Simac "Pastamatic"
Create seven different types of fresh pasta with virtually no effort. Just pour in the flour and other ingredients and watch the motor go to work, producing over a kilo of pasta in under ten minutes. Magic.
STOCKISTS 0171-935 0689

Hamilton Beach Drink Master
Any piece of kitchen equipment with the word "master" in its name has to be a good thing, and this electric milkshake and ice-cream cocktail maker is no exception. To use it, simply flick the button. There's even a control to allow you to vary the thickness of your drinks.
STOCKISTS 0171-349 8411

Gaggia ice-cream maker
With its own freezing system, this *gelatiera* not only makes great ice-cream, but proves less hassle than traipsing down to the shop and stocking up on tubs of vanilla and raspberry ripple. And the in-built mixing blade means you can shovel your own soft fruit straight into the machine.
STOCKISTS 0171-935 0689

Chef's Choice electric knife sharpener
Not only can sharpening knives be bloody hard work, but unless you're an expert, the results are usually pretty disappointing. The electric knife sharpener eliminates both problems, positioning the blade at the optimum angle before restoring the edge to perfection. All without any effort on your part.
STOCKISTS 0171-935 0689

Breville Donut Wizard
Knock up something everyone likes but no one is expecting and your culinary reputation will soar. Enabling you to make six hooped delights at a time, the Wizard is the ultimate in dessert one-upmanship. After all, when was the last time you were offered home-made doughnuts?
STOCKISTS 0161-652 1211

Home Masters "Fresh Hands" Egg
Don't ask us how it works, but wash your hands with this steel egg after cooking and it'll stop your hands whiffing of pungent ingredients. Fish, garlic, onion and prawns are its specialities, which means you can sit straight down to eat after cooking without putting everyone else off with your stinking digits.
STOCKISTS 0171-935 0689

RULES OF STYLE WITH DIGBY CRESCENT

Listen and learn as Digby wades through your queries...

Dear FHM,
Nothing delights me more than cooking. Stir-fries, barbecues, baking my own bread – I'm never happier than when the flour is flying. But what should I wear in the kitchen? All too often, I sit down with guests after several hours of cooking, only to be instantly aware of the splatters of cooking fat on my person. How can I keep clean – and cool – over the hob?

The simple white cotton shirt over a non-pleated pant will pass muster at an informal dinner party, and will keep you from overheating while cooking. But of course, such items will show every spot of extra virgin olive oil. The answer is simple: an apron, my friend. Just be sure to avoid any such items featuring comedy breasts, French maid's outfits or amusing "sayings".

PSC, JIM HENSON PRODUCTIONS. INSET PHOTOGRAPHY: TELEGRAPH COLOUR LIBRARY

There isn't a situation facing the drinking man that can't be sort resolved by donning one of *FHM*'s two faces of masculinity…

LOVER OR

Simply cut out each head and keep about your person. If approached by a beautiful woman, slip on the Hasselhoff "Seduction Head" and allow it to work its magic. However, should a glass-wielding lunatic veer towards you, reach for the Mitchell "Fighting Head" and watch your assailant back off in terror. **WARNING: use of inappropriate head can result in serious injury. Or another lonely night.**

FIGHTER?

"Say that one more time..."

You might be able to give the universal sign for wanker in your local high road when you get cut up by a fat boy in a jeep, but how prepared are you to wind up your foreign foes while on holiday? Use our guide and you'll be able to dish the dirt with the best of them.

■ **Spain** "Me cago en la leche de tu puta madre" *I shit in your whore-mother's milk.* "Que te folle un pez" *May you be fucked by a fish.*

■ **Germany** "Leck mich am Arsch, Hosenscheiser" *Lick my arse, pant-shitter.* "Dir hat wohl jemand ins Gehirn geschissen?" *Has someone shat in your brain, or what?*

■ **Portugal** "Vai mamar na cona da tua mana" *Go suck your mother.*

■ **Australia** "Why don't you stick your dick in your ear and fuck some sense into yourself."

■ **Italy** "Porco Dio" *Pig god.*

■ **Greece** "Na sou skiso don kolo sou" *I will tear your arse apart.* "El adelfi sou gimade me des eyies" *Your sister sleeps with goats.*

■ **Denmark** "Fedte rov" *Sticky-arse.*

■ **Finland** "Veda vittu paahas" *Go pull a vagina over your head.*

■ **Ireland** "O musie, mustais frog arse, o bhitch" *A frog's moustache on you, o bitch.*

■ **France** "Tu ne sais pas plus que de beurre aux fesses" *You don't know buttered buttocks about anything.*

LIFE IMPROVING TIPS

Bidding was brisk at the Goebbels '98 Memorabilia Fair

What's that smell?

Sometimes you know the person you're talking to is lying: the obvious "cheque's in the post" and "we're just good friends" are self-evident falsehoods. But what happens when you're not sure if the shyster you're talking to is telling porkies? Here are several handy tips for the often-duped doofus.

■ **Study hand movements** Liars, like former American President Richard Nixon, will try to add credibility to what they say with enthusiastic gesticulation, in order to distract attention from their lying faces and add false importance to their lies.

■ **Listen to their speech rhythm** When lying, speech is distorted. Sentences leading up to the lie will be rushed, and the speaker may stutter and emphasise wrong words.

■ **Test their memory** Lies are used to get out of a tight spot and are quickly forgotten. All you have to do is ask the liar what they've just said, and more often than not they'll have forgotten the exact phrase.

■ **Listen to their tone of voice** When lying, the pitch or volume will alter. If a punk gets squeaky, you can bet your bottom dollar he's talking through his arse.

■ **Check for eye contact** People who are lying find it hard to retain eye contact. A glance to one side can be very revealing, and often occurs when the liar hits the main part of his fabrication.

■ **Excess detail and fact are a give-away** A liar will try to make a story sound memorable. If the story you are being told is complex and detail-ridden, it is probably manufactured. Most people don't remember *everything*.

■ **Heavy perspiration, regardless of weather conditions** When the pressure is on, the sweat starts to flow. Beads of perspiration on the forehead are the obvious giveaway, but don't forget to watch out for examples of more subtle migrating dampness due south of the armpits.

Maxwell: no match for Hasselhoff

HOW TO SELL A SECOND-HAND CAR

"One careful owner, runs like new..."

Getting rid of the most expensive piece of machinery you'll ever own is a tricky business. The used car market is prowled by sharks, and every bit of inside info you can garner is invaluable. Follow some of our tips and you should get the best price for your motor.

■ **Compete price-wise** Know the market. A good reference is *The Black Book* produced by the Confidential Auto Prices: although you can't buy this volume (only dealers can), if you can get a peek at it you'll know the best price you can get away with.

■ **Make sure the car looks good** A clean and polished vehicle will be easier to shift than one that looks clapped out. It's also a good idea to respray the car if it's a dodgy colour: blue and red cars sell a lot better

The Toxteth Park 'N' Ride scheme was short-lived

than beige ones. Vacuum the inside and make sure the car doesn't stink.

■ **Place lots of ads** While the press and local media are obvious targets, consider Videotron, which is an advertising-only cable channel. And don't be shy about sticking a card in the window of the car with a price and phone number.

■ **Ensure that it sounds desirable** Lie a little – this way there is likely to be at least some interest. Go through other adverts for cars and look at the language they use: "potential classic", for example, doesn't actually mean anything, but it sounds good.

■ **Get rid of rust** Use an 8lb tin of filler, some sandpaper and a sprayer who knows what he's doing. This will push up the car's value and ease the sale.

■ **Replace cheap parts and check the paperwork** A full service history will bolster your motor's value, and take care over the details – make sure such things as interior lightbulbs are working.

■ **Use the auctions** As long as the vehicle looks good, starts and runs okay, it will sell. At an auction, the pressure's on the buyers, who only get one chance to give the cars a once-over before they have to bid.

LIFE IMPROVING TIPS

HOW TO BEAT STRESS

Just count to ten...

It gets us all in the end. The Big S. Some of us break out in hives and sweat a lot. Some of us lose our hair. Some of us simply keel over with a massive heart attack. Stress is just part of life, but while we can't eliminate it entirely, we can try to manage it, and recognise when it starts to tighten an oily hand around our hearts.

■ **Watch yourself** The main causes of stress are money, work, love, health and bereavement. So, basically, you're going to have stress at some point in your life. The key is to be aware of when it is happening. If you start to feel strange two weeks after the funeral of your mother, think about how you are dealing with grief.

■ **Pay attention to early warnings** Immense stress build-up may result in a heart attack. This occurs as arteries narrow due to wear and tear from the "flight" hormone released in response to stress. Avoid being overambitious or overworking, but also watch for pain, tiredness, shortness of breath and hot and cold flushes.

■ **Look after your body** A fit body will be able to deal with the physical aspects of stress better than a strung-out, hard-smoking, alcoholic wreck. Eat properly – hard workers only find time for junk food. Ulcers may occur and weight increase. Cut down on alcohol. Stop smoking. Exercise.

■ **Watch key indicators** There are many indicators of stress. You may start drinking more to deal with a situation; you may start smoking heavily. Many people begin using drugs – either anti-depressants or stimulants – when under pressure. This may result in addiction, sleep-loss, migraines, damage to the immune system, depression and impotence.

■ **Take time out** It is important to find the time to relax. Do not allow your work to get on top of you. Exercise, eat well and take care of yourself.

The Simon Weston-a-gram was a real showstopper

STEVE McCURRY/MAGNUM, KOBAL

"BEGONE, GOD

There's about a million Jehovah's Witnesses in the world – and they don't think that's enough. But here's how to put a dent in their evangelical zeal

EVERYONE LIKES TO MAKE OUT that they're highly skilled at out-witting Jehovah's Witnesses, but when religious canvassers actually knock on the door our repartee is pretty pathetic. Either we nod politely for a couple of minutes, take a leaflet and promise we'll read about Armageddon once we've finished the washing-up, or we slam the door in their faces and only moan about the cheek of people waking us up to tell us about our shortcomings when they're out of earshot.

Neither of these responses is going to deter the gleamy-toothed freaks from coming back. No, to make absolutely sure the Witnesses never return, you'll have to convince them you're more of a nutter than

QUICK-FIRE METHODS

When time's of the essence, use one of these proven techniques

1 Pretend to be deaf. If the Witnesses then start thrusting booklets into your hand, feign blindness as well.
2 Pretend to be on the phone when they ring the bell, and gesture to them that you'll be there in a minute. Stay on the phone as long as it takes for them to go away, repeating the "almost ready" gesture every couple of minutes if you really want to get their backs up.
3 Speak to them in a made-up language, wagging your finger angrily for extra effect.
4 Answer the door carrying a poker, with ketchup dripping down your chin. If you have a dog, respond to its frenzied barking from the kitchen with the order: "Put her down, Satan!"
5 Reply to the introduction "We're Jehovah's Witnesses" with "Brilliant. I'm Jehovah. Come on in."

they are. Naturally, this requires some effort. Our best models are other religious people, who over the years have built up a massive scriptural armoury to combat the cult canvasser; mix their arguments with some simple pagan abuse – to make sure the Witness doesn't start enjoying the exchange of doctrinal banter – and you'll soon be rid of them. Run through these five techniques in order and they'll be scurrying next door before you can say Hallelujah.

Step one Start with a gentle jibe. Point out that the second leader of the Jehovah's Witnesses was a bloke called Joseph Rutherford, who was so convinced the end of the world was nigh that he bought a house in San Diego and had the deeds made out to Noah, Isaac, David, Gideon and Joshua. Suggest that if biblical characters were capable of coming back from the dead, they should be able to sort out their own accommodation.

Step two A bit of a technical point this, but certainly worth a shot. According to the Witnesses, Jesus Christ was executed on a stake with both hands over his head. But their own version of the Bible states that the phrase "Jesus, King Of The Jews" was posted on a sign directly above his head. If his hands were above his head, how did they fit the sign there as well? As they try to explain this, doubtless excited by the prospect of a debate, look blank for a second and then, with a dreamy look, mutter: "Personally, I prefer beheading. That way you get to see the brains."

Jebediah's final exam was going fine until he came to the Killing Room

Step three By now, they'll be confused. At first you looked like you understood the movement's history and were willing to engage in a discussion, and now it seems you've turned hostile. Reinforce both impressions by yelling one of the following dates at the very top of your voice every

Convince them that you're more of a nutter than they are...

-BOTHERER!"

Cub Scouts Small boys are immensely insecure about having to wear stupid uniforms. Open the door, start laughing, and tell them only dickheads wear short trousers and woggles. They will run.

Salesmen Anyone peddling goods door-to-door is primed for rejection: a polite "no thank you" will never deter them. So, even before you've established what they're selling, tell them that you'll buy the lot. When they murmur a protest, question their professional integrity with an impatient cry of "Look, do you want a sale or not?" Then frantically scribble down a telephone number, preferably prefixed with the code for Dubai (00 9714), and tell them your accountant will sort out everything.

Trick-or-treaters The great thing about these kids is that you can be sure – give or take an hour or two – of exactly when they'll arrive. So, on the afternoon of October 31, post a notice on your door explaining that "EXTORTIONISTS WILL BE PROSECUTED". The kids will come to your door and pause for a second as they attempt to understand what the notice means, allowing you to pour freezing water on them from an upstairs window while screaming: "Trick! Trick! Trick!"

The milkman who wants a bonus at Christmas Really underhand measures are required here. Tell him you're a Jehovah's Witness and you can't celebrate a birthday, even if it's that of Jesus, and offer to explain your creed to him over breakfast. Desperate to escape, he'll make his excuses, forgetting all about his tip.

time they start a sentence: 1914, 1925 and 1975. According to *Watchtower* magazine, all three years were supposed to have ushered in the end of the world.

Step four If that doesn't shift the door-steppers, put a party hat on your head. Explain how happy you are that they've come round to congratulate you on your birthday, especially as all your friends have forgotten the occasion. Jehovah's Witnesses are forbidden to celebrate birthdays, so they'll begin to shuffle uncomfortably. When they fail to congratulate you, start screaming that your mother died giving birth to you and your father was killed in a car crash on the way to the hospital. Get on your knees and mournfully sing *Happy Birthday* to yourself over and over again.

Step five If they've not gone by now, you've got your work cut out. Invite them in, sit them down and prep the video for Tommy Lee and Pam Anderson's home porn movie. Say you're going to brew some tea then go and hide, hoping they'll leave in disgust. But if they haven't budged, surprise them with a Polaroid and tell them you know where their elders live. You've won either way.

"YOU LOOK RAVISHING, MY LOVE"

HAL in *2001* couldn't lie, and went mad. But you can... and should!

Everyone loved Mavis's collar and handbag combo. Eventually

SUBJECT	YOU WANT TO SAY	YOU PROBABLY SAY	YOU SHOULD HAVE SAID
Your girlfriend's been piling on the pounds recently. "Am I getting fat?" she asks.	"Yes you are, you old tugboat. Get slim or I'll leave you for someone thinner."	"Oh no! I'll always fancy you no matter how you look, love."	"You've put on a little weight. Are *you* happy with it?" Then, if she continues to bloat up and you stop fancying her, she can't say: "But you never even told me."
You've been in a drunken punch-up with some rival football fans. Your girl wants to know why you're covered in blood.	"I did him good and proper! I just wish you'd been there to see it."	"I fell over."	"A woman was being bothered by some drunks. I stepped in to help and one of them clocked me." She'll be fawning over you like a child that's scratched his knee.
You've missed work because you had a hangover, and your boss is quizzing you the day you return.	"Actually, I spent the first part of the day watching TV, the second half masturbating, then I went out at night. What are you going to do about it?"	"I was really sick. It must have been a 24-hour bug or something."	"I vomited throughout the day and my faeces were spotted with blood," you say, as he turns green. Next, apply the *coup de grace*: "Then came the rectal leak..."
You don't earn an awful lot, but your mates think you're doing alright... until one of them demands the truth at a party.	"Look, I'm earning a pittance. Happy now?"	"I'm doing okay, you know. I could earn more if I worked for a rival company, but I'm happy."	"I leave the facts and figures at the office, mate. I'm not exactly starving, as you can see, so let's have a drink and enjoy ourselves, okay?"
Your girlfriend asks how many people you've slept with. The truth – be it shedloads or pitiably few – is going to hurt someone...	"Yeah, and damn good they were, too. In fact, I think about them all when we're doing it. Honest!"	"You know, the average really, not too many... Oh, is the football on?"	"The others have paled into insignificance since I've been seeing you. I'm not going to tell you how many, because you'll tell me your figure and I'll get dead jealous."
Your mate is dating a whining, moaning harpie. "What do you think of her?" he says one night.	"Oh, I wish you hadn't asked me that. She's an ugly, cantankerous old slag, and you're a loser for putting up with her."	"Yeah, I really like her. She's nice. You're a lucky man, you are."	"I'm happy if you're happy. She may not be my cup of tea, but then look at the dogs I chase!" Let him know she's not perfect and move quickly on.
You've just seen a film on a friend's recommendation. It was rubbish.	"I've never been so bored in all my born days. If you thought that was good, you're not getting out much, you loser. Reimburse my admission fee, please."	"It was quite good, really."	"Maybe I was missing something..." It's important to be honest here: never let yourself be judged by your apparent love of what you *know* is wrong.
Your friend's had a baby and you bump into him in the street, pram in tow. The kid is hideous...	"What an ugly little critter you've produced."	"My, isn't it sweet. Mother's eyes, definitely."	"Winston Churchill? Only joking! Very distinctive features." Never dis a baby: the parents, groggy from lack of sleep, always think it's the dog's bollocks.
Your girlfriend's just brought home something she's made at pottery classes. It's as bad as the blind girl's bust of Lionel Ritchie.	"Christ! It looks like Stephen Hawking's been at the potter's wheel!"	"Nice. That's really... nice."	"That's a very thought-provoking piece. It would look great in the spare room." You don't want to upset her, but praise may lead to further kiln-fired abortions.
Your woman asks you if you love her. You don't, although the sex is good, and nothing better has come along.	"No I don't, and I never will."	"Of course I do, my sweet love."	"You've turned my heart inside out. 'I love you' doesn't encapsulate everything you mean to me." Don't say anything but this. Just don't, no matter what. Don't.

KOBAL

THE BAD HAIR GUIDE

Few things are as traumatic as a bad haircut. Take consolation in the fact that many men have the same miserable barnet as you...

The mullet: number one among rednecks

THE BOX CUT/QUIFF
The shorter the box cut (or flat top), the more it was supposed to resemble the rugged cut of a US Marine. The longer it got, the more it looked like Morrissey's barmy barnet – and everyone knows that he never got laid.
Guilty parties: anyone in *Top Gun*.

THE FRENCH CROP
George Michael started the trend for the French crop during his *Listen Without Prejudice* period, but it was quickly imitated by barbers unable to recreate the look with the same degree of accuracy, leaving customers with straggly strands scraped over the forehead.
Guilty parties: George Michael; the dark-haired ugly geek from teen sensations 911.

THE PERM
Demi-, semi-, Remi Moses... whatever the perm, it's simply not acceptable. If your hair is straight then live with it, and work with what you've got. Any experimentation with the curling tongs and you'll inevitably end up looking like a) the younger, more stupid brother of Terry McDermott, or b) your mum.
Guilty parties: Any Liverpool player in the late Seventies; all of Earth, Wind And Fire.

THE MOHAWK
This shorter version of the Mohican was worn by men who couldn't be arsed to grow their hair long. They thought it made them look like tough. It didn't. It made them look like they'd stuck a strip of Axminster to their bonces.
Guilty party: Robert De Niro in *Taxi Driver*.

THE RAT-TAIL
This heinous haircut was actually declared illegal in the state of Missouri in 1983: anyone found walking the streets sporting this style is liable to a spot fine of $100, and persistent offenders can find themselves with a six-month jail sentence. In Mediterranean countries, however, the rat-tail is considered a sign of a man's virility.
Guilty parties: Greek bodybuilders.

SHAVEN SIDES
Sinister Gothic style whereby the long hair, inevitably dyed jet-black, is maintained, but the hair above the ears and at the base of the hair-line is shaved upward. Made worse, if possible, when the wearer's ginger roots clearly begin to show through.
Guilty parties: Any one of the pasty-faced pricks in The Mission.

HIGHLIGHTS
Peer in the window of any two-bit barbers in the country and you'll notice the same black-and-white pictures of faintly effeminate men in the window, with haircuts the crimper inside could never hope to emulate. You'll also notice that they all have highlights. Is it just coincidence that each and every one of them looks like Vera Duckworth?
Guilty parties: Dollar's David Van Day; George Michael in *Careless Whisper* phase.

THE MULLET
The haircut the Devil would have sported if he wasn't just a device used by the Catholic Church to scare the pants off the weak-willed. Long at the back, short on top and the choice of cut for every redneck retard over the pond. Quite simply, the most offensive hairdo in the known world.
Guilty parties: Mel Gibson; Rod Stewart; any American bloke aged 14 to 23.

THE WEDGE
A catastrophic cut, favoured by the likes of David Sylvian and the other fops in Japan. Floppy on top and shaved up the back, it's a truly appalling vision of nastiness, often compounded by a tint or lo-light.
Guilty parties: Each and every suited and booted member of Modern Romance.

THE FLICK
Found favour in the mid-Eighties among fey, introspective bands such as A Flock Of Seagulls, the members of which all looked like girls. A proper flick should cover one eye entirely, *à la* Gabrielle.
Guilty parties: Human League frontman Phil Oakey, circa 1983.

MICK HUTSON

WYOMING
Fact It's a crime to encourage someone else to masturbate.
Danger of arrest If you're caught with a jazz mag, you'll be okay – but the editor gets prosecuted.

NEW YORK
Fact Adultery is a crime.
Danger of arrest Low, but a couple recently faced prosecution when the woman's husband took pictures of her and her lover frolicking. Best hide all cameras after planning your tryst.

SWITZERLAND
Fact It's a crime to co-habit.
Danger of arrest If you make a point of appearing unmarried (having loud sex, acting like you're in love): high. In one district, more than 20 couples have been fined.

KANSAS
Fact Vibrators and other sex toys are illegal.
Danger of arrest High. In 1982, a man was arrested selling blow-up dolls, and there have been many convictions since. Sex aids are equals of Class-A drugs.

WASHINGTON DC
Fact It's a crime to give or receive oral sex.
Danger of arrest If your name's Bill Clinton, slight. Otherwise, it would have to be an ex pissed off with your technique who shops you to the boys in blue.

ENGLAND/WALES
Fact Buggery is a crime.
Danger of arrest Minimal – someone has to report you, or you have to tell a copper yourself. In 1971, a man accidentally did this while discussing another offence with the cops – and got 18 months.

SEX WITHOUT FRONTIERS!

Tuck this alongside the tanning butter when packing for your hols...

PSC KA7 KORAI

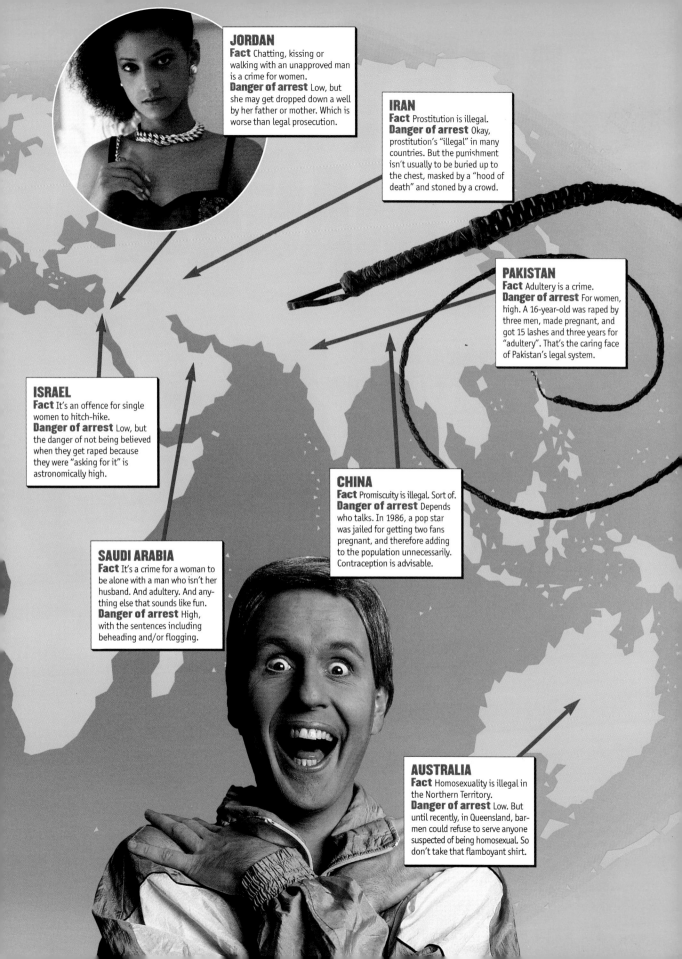

JORDAN
Fact Chatting, kissing or walking with an unapproved man is a crime for women.
Danger of arrest Low, but she may get dropped down a well by her father or mother. Which is worse than legal prosecution.

IRAN
Fact Prostitution is illegal.
Danger of arrest Okay, prostitution's "illegal" in many countries. But the punishment isn't usually to be buried up to the chest, masked by a "hood of death" and stoned by a crowd.

PAKISTAN
Fact Adultery is a crime.
Danger of arrest For women, high. A 16-year-old was raped by three men, made pregnant, and got 15 lashes and three years for "adultery". That's the caring face of Pakistan's legal system.

ISRAEL
Fact It's an offence for single women to hitch-hike.
Danger of arrest Low, but the danger of not being believed when they get raped because they were "asking for it" is astronomically high.

CHINA
Fact Promiscuity is illegal. Sort of.
Danger of arrest Depends who talks. In 1986, a pop star was jailed for getting two fans pregnant, and therefore adding to the population unnecessarily. Contraception is advisable.

SAUDI ARABIA
Fact It's a crime for a woman to be alone with a man who isn't her husband. And adultery. And anything else that sounds like fun.
Danger of arrest High, with the sentences including beheading and/or flogging.

AUSTRALIA
Fact Homosexuality is illegal in the Northern Territory.
Danger of arrest Low. But until recently, in Queensland, barmen could refuse to serve anyone suspected of being homosexual. So don't take that flamboyant shirt.

MAKE YOUR OWN MAGAZINE

Too tight to buy your own *FHM*? Then glue your own together!

DIRTY NAILS " "

BALD WOMEN!

Sombreros !!!!!!!

SEX!

Shoot

Rocket!! " "

" "

Love your acne

Travel to DiscWorld with Terry Gilliam

WEAK CHINS " "

SEX!

Monkey-gland lager

BOLSHY GITS!

Buried alive for sixteen years!

PLUS

I STINK BAD!

" "

FHM

PLUS

God **Stiff**

oh

SEX!

" "

¡SEX!

" "

Hot

VOYAGE INTO
YOUR ARSE!

Gain muscles
in hours!

My girlfriend dumped
me for her mother!

How to cook
your pet

**PLASTIC
TEETH**

" "

THIN ANKLES

Crazed!

SEX!

Gewankenhurst!

SEX!

Interview with a corpse

Eat more and still
lose weight!

**I THINK I'VE
KILLED MY
GIRLFRIEND**

coma

NEW
RELIGIONS!

**MY LIFE
AS A DOG**

Elderly relatives often baulk at some of *FHM*'s "raunchy" covers. To save their blushes, simply use this free, cut-out-and-keep *FHM* slip-cover...

FHM

IT'S A VICTORIAN THING

JANUARY 1899 ONE FARTHING

EXOTIC TRAVEL!

Brighton, Blackpool and Whitley Bay

EMMELINE AND AMY PANKHURST
What the butler didn't see

SAUCY JACK
Can anyone stop the Ripper?

HEAVY METAL THUNDER!
Special fold-out poster of Brunel's new bridge

"BY GEORGE, MR STEPHENSON! THAT'S ONE HECK OF A LOCOMOTIVE!"
On the fast track with the Rocket

"MAY I BE SO BOLD?"
Courting advice from the not-so-gentle men

THE GREAT EXHIBITION
Mousetrap opens

PLUS!
Scullery maids on the sofa, WG Grace, wax that moustache, side parting vs the centre, walking sticks, Houdini, the Crimea and pocket watches

CRIPES!

Anne gets us hot under the collar

HOW TO GET A PAY RISE
Take it to the bank

Workers of the world, unite! No matter what you are being paid, you are worth more. The only problem is convincing the people who pay you that this is the case. Next time you go in to talk to the breadheads who own your very soul, take our handy guide with you and you'll come out a richer man.

■ **Don't bully your boss** Demanding a rise is no good. You must be reasonable – give and take. Storming in, laying down the law, only works in the movies; in real life, you'll put your boss on the defensive.

■ **Appearance is all important** The right clothes and attitude will only enhance your chances of success.

Looking like a poverty-stricken wreck won't evoke sympathy – only contempt.

■ **Pick the right moment** It is essential that your boss is in a good mood. Do not ask for a rise just after losing a major client, or when your boss has decided to divorce his wife.

■ **Ask for more than you want** This way, you'll be able to reduce the figure, and thus pretend you are willing to compromise. Why not go to the pub and buy your boss lots of drinks? You never know, when he's pissed, the old man might not realise what he has just agreed to.

■ **Write a letter from another firm offering you**

Magoo Jnr filled his swag bags with kittens

more money If you're a valued member of staff, your boss won't want you buggering off to a rival. Just make sure he never finds out you were lying.

■ **Prove your worth** Work well and be impressive. This way you can show you deserve a rise. Just prior to asking for a load of money, work really hard and put in extra hours. Look in

adverts to compare your salary with others in the market to justify your request.

■ **Don't put it off** It seems like a daunting task asking your boss for "a few minutes". A good manager will not laugh or bite your head off. Put forward a good case and you'll wish you'd asked earlier.

HOW TO GIVE AN EROTIC MASSAGE
You've got the touch

While it is all very well to occasionally have caveman sex – in and out in under 60 seconds – your lady might prefer it if you spent a little longer in the pre-coital sensual mode. In fact, she might not want sex at all: women, it seems, actually prefer a full-on body massage without the added bonus of sex!

■ **Set the atmosphere** A bit of romance can go a long way. Candles or soft lighting are essential. Burn some incense, play the right music.

■ **Use props** Oils will ensure smoothness and extra pleasure, while later you may have some fun with feathers or more exotic toys. You can prepare the ground by buying your girl some skimpy lingerie, then peel it off as you mould her body into a ball of desire.

■ **Clip your nails and remove rings** It's better that the screams are of pleasure, not of pain. Make sure your hands remain

The clothes thief was determined to nab Sue's headband

in contact with her skin. Take your time – make her feel wanted. Be gentle; press too hard and she'll be covered in bruises. To relieve tension, focus on neck, shoulders and upper back. Straddle her and gently press her shoulders. This helps her get used to the feeling of your hands on her skin.

■ **Warm her back** Massage her back with a flat hand, fingers together. Move hands in parallel lines up either side of her spine – do not press directly on it – then move out across her shoulders and down the sides of her torso. Spread your fingers, keeping them somewhat stiff, and rake them down her back from shoulders to buttocks. This releases deep, underlying tissue tension.

■ **Move onto her lower back** This area can be congested and tender – especially in pre-menstrual women. Lightly massage this area with small circular strokes on her buttocks, hips and upper thighs. To focus on sexual energy, give special attention to her release points – the neck and ears.

■ **Feet are important** The whole body may be soothed from the foot. Do not tickle – this will only result in a painful kick.

LIFE IMPROVING TIPS

COCK GAUGE POUCH ▷

Under no circumstances should any sane man with enough money to dress himself wear pants which measure his manhood. And don't think you can get away with stuffing a wad of tissues down the end.

THE SLOGAN PANT ▽

Having a motto on the lines of "Bigshot" with a picture of a cannon on your pants says to anyone who sees you undress: "Here is a man who probably draws in biro on his arm and wipes his nose on his jumper cuffs." Sad.

SMALL DISASTERS

Truly, a man's pant is the very window to his soul

RED SATIN POUCH ▽

It's red. It's satin. It has brass studs on it, for Christ's sake. What woman is going to be impressed with static and the possibility of scratch-marks all over her belly? She'll think: "He's cheap. He's nasty. I'm leaving."

TINY BLACK TANGA ▷

Girls, it's true, can get away with g-strings, tangas and thongs. Men, unless they are German, appearing in a porn film and don't care, should never wear anything which rides up their arse and restricts the tackle.

◁ PATTERNED BRIEFS

There's a good reason why white, grey and black pants were invented: patterns looking more at home on a pub wall are strictly for blokes who still live with their mum and play Subbuteo. On their own.

RULES OF STYLE WITH DIGBY CRESCENT

Listen and learn as Digby wades through your queries...

Dear FHM,

I was recently asked to go the swimming baths by a young lady I've just met. And, eager to impress her with my artificial tan and finely-toned physique, I thought I might sport a less-is-more-style trunk. But then a friend rained on my parade by suggesting that a skimpy swimmer is more likely to put her off than turn her on. What should I do?

Under no circumstances should the trunk be employed in this day and age. Barring its adoption by Chris Quentin and the travelling cricketer, this is a garment best left alone. And as women have found, it's sometimes better to hint at what's to come than reveal the sometimes startling truth. Go for the swimming short, my friend.

The Dibnahs
despaired of
ever letting
Fred's old room

FLAT SHARE HELL

Setting up in a place of your own should be an occasion of deep joy. However, if you choose the wrong people to share with, your dream home could become a Hammer House of Horror. Don't get caught out – here's how to spot the world's worst flatshare buddies… ▷

KOBAL

By the time Ted woke up, Woodstock was all over

Evict flatshare pests – legally

The pressures of flat-sharing can, and probably will, drive you stark staring mad. Whether this is down to someone stealing the last of the milk every morning or because you have to put up with unsavoury smells and unreasonable noise is unimportant; what you want to know is, what can you do get rid of an unwanted pest?

The one thing you must not do is hassle an unwelcome housemate. "Your co-tenant has rights," the Law Society says. "If they haven't actually broken the law or breached their contract, they have the right to live as they please."

Sadly, there's not much you can do if they have signed a contract and aren't breaking any of its clauses. And if they do break a contract, you'll still have to drag them through the courts, which takes time. But fortunately, most rental agreements are now so complex that almost any behaviour can be deemed worthy of eviction, from failing to clean the windows to playing electronic equipment after 11pm.

All you really have to do is complain to your landlord, and he should warn the offending party. If they persist in behaving badly he should serve them notice, and they have to leave. Remember, however, that this all takes months of to-ing and fro-ing. Far better to talk to the pest, urge them to get out and have a replacement tenant ready to fill the gap, thereby ensuring that the landlord gets his rent – which is all he's interested in anyway.

THE ENTHUSIAST

Danger signs Anyone who has a serious hobby should be treated with caution when entering into communal living. Turning up at a new house and finding your co-lodger on the steps with a full drum kit should ring alarm bells. And the presence of glass tanks with living creatures inside them should also see you making your excuses and leaving.

How to get rid of him... *Undermine his enthusiasm and try to get him interested in something less annoying. Is this fails, stage a burglary and have his hobby gear nicked.*

THE UNKEMPT

Danger signs It's true that some scruffs have a certain roguish attraction, but this is usually pretty superficial. What isn't superficial is the ability for one seriously unhygienic person to make an entire three-storey house smell of rancid feet. Watch out for salt-stained armpits, things moving in the hair and any unrecognisable body odours.

How to get rid of him... *Attack. Hide week-old kippers under his floorboards and stink him out of your life.*

THE SEX ADDICT

Danger signs Moving in with a loose woman seems like a great idea – loads of uncomplicated drunken sex and a quick stagger back to your room afterwards – but what happens when her unquenchable sexual appetites start to wear you down? Where do you go to hide? Will you be able to put up with her banging an endless stream of losers from the pub?

How to get rid of her... *You've got two choices: make your sexual demands so bizarre that she gets worried (tell her you want to let an animal share in your lust); or tell her you absolutely must have a child with her soon.*

THE SURVIVALIST

Danger signs You're moving in. Your co-tenant pulls up in a battered Land Rover and unloads his cardboard boxes. Have a peak inside: if they're weighed down with tins of food, powdered egg, oil lamps, catapults, bottled water and generators, you could be sharing with a doom merchant waiting for the collapse of civilisation.

How to get rid of him... *Be positive. Tell him how optimistic you are and that you're really looking forward to the millennium. Fill the living room with flowers. Bring young relatives round to look at his "funny room". He will be unnerved, and soon leave.*

THE TELLY ADDICT

Danger signs "Hello mate," your new flattie says as you carry in his cheese plant. "Did you catch the re-run of *The Hit Man And Her* last night? Fucking seminal that was. You know Michela Stratton? She's on satellite now..." Without fail, he'll also be a slightly deaf insomniac. How long do you think that trying to get to sleep while *Prisoner: Cell Block H* bangs out will remain endearing?

How to get rid of him... *Use electrical equipment which causes interference on his set, and constantly adjust the colour, contrast and vertical hold so that the picture is unwatchable, then tell him you think it's crystal clear.*

The young Jimmy Hill loved a lager

THE SPORTS FREAK

Danger signs Nobody minds sharing with someone they can watch the match with, or even share a few frames of World Championship snooker, but what if your flatmate is obsessed with all forms of sport? If every conversation veers towards the relative merits of bowls over curling, or whether shinty should revise its outmoded offside law, you'd better think about parting ways.

How to get rid of him... *Make it very clear that you think all varieties of competition are the mark of capitalist running dogs, and that, as a committed socialist, you can't possibly take an interest in such oppressive activities.*

SOCIAL BUTTERFLIES

Danger signs Within 15 minutes of moving in the telephone is ringing off the hook and huge crowds of people come

round for coffee, pre-pub drinks, post-pub drinks, poetry evenings, drama classes, *ER* sessions and long, drawn-out foody gatherings. You, essentially, are an inconvenience who is allowed to hang around occasionally and clean up the mess.

How to get rid of them... *Recruit your own social crowd, but invite the lads from the pub football team. The subsequent clash of interests will inevitably end in tears. Or bloodshed.*

THE STRUGGLING ARTIST

Danger signs The fevered brow, the unshaven chin, the fag ash peppered down the front of the shirt, the huge boxes of yellowing manuscripts. Do you really think you can survive the angst your flatmate suffers when yet another rejection slip drops onto the mat, and he is driven to fretting, booze and crowing for sympathy?

How to get rid of him... *Get a vanity publisher to produce your own book, then brag mercilessly. The sheer humiliation of living with a published novelist will soon have him running for a garret of his own.*

ECOLOGISTS

Danger signs Every product in the house will have to be biodegradable, from the washing-up liquid to the toilet paper. Food will run the full range from lentils to couscous, and protest workshops against the ruination of the rainforest and eating Big Macs will become the highlight of the week.

How to get rid of them... *Bring home a whole cow carcass for tea, indulge your aerosol deodorant habit to the hilt and buy products which come in a pointless and wasteful amount of packaging.*

THE PARTY ANIMAL

Danger signs If, on first inspection of your new living room, you're greeted by a bloke with a huge gut waving his fist in the air and making ape noises as he chugs a can of lager through a hole in the base of the tin, then you're sharing with a party bore. Have a peek at his video collection: if it contains the horribly over-rated *Blues Brothers*, be prepared for an endless, dreary, repetitive round of "partying".

How to get rid of him... *Post faked letters from the local Environmental Health Department threatening huge fines and possible imprisonment if the noise doesn't stop.*

The geographers were behind with the rent again

"IS IT SERIOUS, DOCTOR?"

We trawl the world's hospital wards for the most gruesome medical conditions known to man…

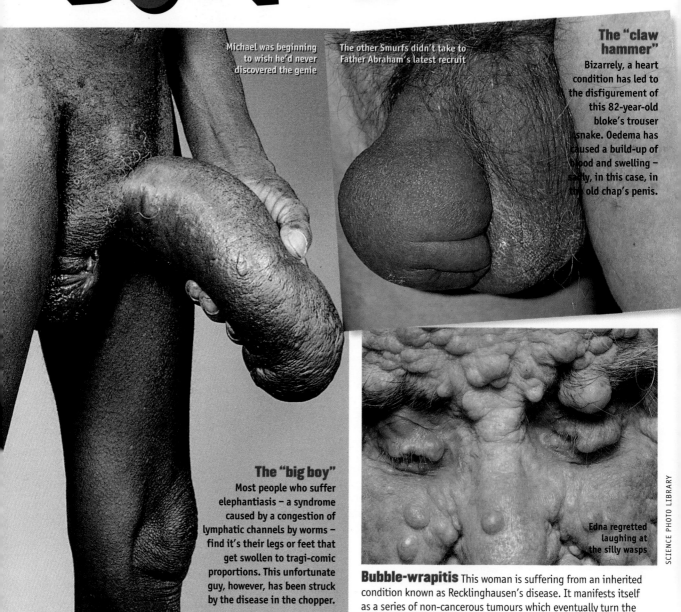

Michael was beginning to wish he'd never discovered the genie

The other Smurfs didn't take to Father Abraham's latest recruit

The "claw hammer"
Bizarrely, a heart condition has led to the disfigurement of this 82-year-old bloke's trouser snake. Oedema has caused a build-up of blood and swelling – sadly, in this case, in the old chap's penis.

The "big boy"
Most people who suffer elephantiasis – a syndrome caused by a congestion of lymphatic channels by worms – find it's their legs or feet that get swollen to tragi-comic proportions. This unfortunate guy, however, has been struck by the disease in the chopper.

Edna regretted laughing at the silly wasps

SCIENCE PHOTO LIBRARY

Bubble-wrapitis This woman is suffering from an inherited condition known as Recklinghausen's disease. It manifests itself as a series of non-cancerous tumours which eventually turn the victim's face into a disgusting boil-riddled mess.

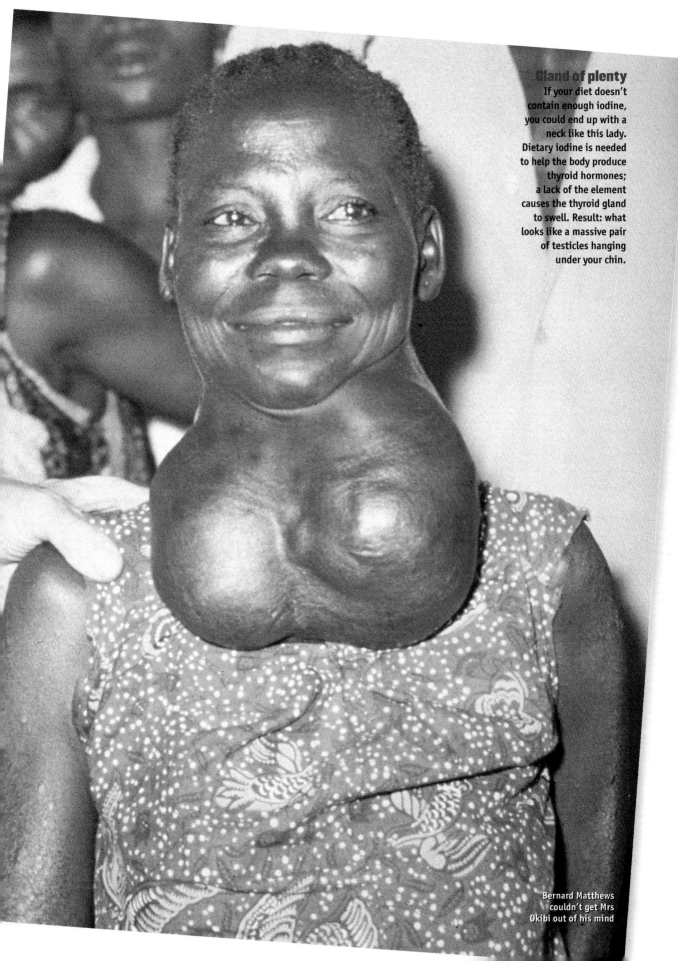

Bernard Matthews
couldn't get Mrs
Okibi out of his mind

READ ALL ABOUT HER!

All you have to do is notice what magazine she has by the bed, and react accordingly to her needs…

COSMOPOLITAN

Who the magazine wants you to think reads it Sussed, Nineties chicks who can move seamlessly from boardroom to bedroom, while staying in touch with their emotions and coming to terms with the reality of equal (sexual!) relationships. Plus they know that this summer, exfoliation is a beauty must, and that friends are the new family.

Who really reads it Bored secretaries who think it'll tell them how to Get That Job, and who fondly believe they can do "The Most Important Love Test – Ever!" on you by adding your moon sign and your age together and dividing it by six.
How to impress her Say: "You know, it's hard being a Nineties man. We forget how vital it can be to take a dip in Lake Me sometimes. But not as hard as it is being a woman who knows she can Have It All." Then grin boyishly and give her the loan of your chunky-knit sweater.

ELLE

Who the magazine wants you to think reads it The cream of international society, as they relax on long-haul flights planning which Jill Sander top will wittily complement that Prada skirt, and smiling in recognition at the feisty opinions of the magazine's columnists.
Who reads it: Underpaid PR women who hope that by wittily mixing a Miss Selfridge boob tube with a M&S mini, they'll be mistaken for Patsy Kensit. Even though they live in Romford, they fantasise about grooving in the streets of London – unaware that Soho is full of irritable motorcycle couriers and Japanese tourists, not Stella McCartney's laughing friends.
How to impress her: Say: "I must sort out my relationship with my father, before I end up like Blake Morrison. I was talking to Patrick – yeah, Cox – the other day, and he said Pharmacy's so *passé*. The only really interesting space in London is Tracey Emin's new installation."

MORE!

Who the magazine wants you to think reads it Good-time girls in groovy, metropolitan

jobs, who share a brightly-painted flat and like a bottle of chilled white wine and hot sex with their men even more than a holiday to Ibiza with ten close female mates and a suitcase full of erotic novels.
Who really reads it Fat, 13-year-old schoolgirls whose mums would go mad if they knew their daughter was reading about Position Of The Fortnight – but will never find out because she keeps it at school so she and her mates can shriek with longing over it every break-time.
How to impress her Say: "Yeah, I left school ages ago. My job's quite cool, actually, I get to meet loads of pop stars and that. I could get you Will Mellor's autograph, you know. Put on lots of make-up, try and look 18, and I might be able to sneak you in to a nightclub." Then put on a Pete Tong remix tape.

PRIMA

Who the magazine wants you to think reads it Women in control of their busy lives, who can rustle up some soup as easily as knit a Postman Pat sweater, who care about the health of their kids and the need to provide an imaginative cold supper at short notice, and can still maintain shiny, glossy hair.

Who really reads it Bored housewives who find it pleasant to fantasise about the soups they could rustle up if only they had the right blender, and single women who, more than anything, want a man to cook and care for and a happy band of children wearing matching cable-knit sweaters in different colourways... rather than thinking about the soul-sapping job they have to do and the micro-meals for one they find themselves hunched over nightly.

How to impress her Cultivate a vulnerable, unkempt charm, while reminding her of your highly-paid job and lack of anyone satisfyingly unambitious with whom to share the benefits. Ask her if she'll cook for you, then say with a grin: "Did I tell you what my six-year-old cousin said? It was so cute!"

VOGUE
Who the magazine wants you to think reads it Rich, glamorous, intelligent women, who care

about fashion in an intellectual way and can afford to treat themselves to Gucci coats and D&G corsets on a regular basis, while all the time arranging supper parties at the country house and booking themselves into Ayurvedic spas in Tibet to escape the stress of shopping and attending charity events.

Who really reads it Women who want other people on trains to think they're glamorous, who buy designer clothes at Discount Retail Outlets, dream of having their hair cut by Nicky Clarke, who feverishly scan the social pages to see if they can lay claim to knowing anyone passing in the background of the photos, and who keep all their shopping bags for display purposes.

How to impress her Say: "God, Aspen was heaving this year, it's not what it was, and the bloody button came off my Richard James suit when I was in First Class trying to unwind. It's so exhausting being asked to put in appearances at charity bashes all the time, but one *does* feels obliged." Then look at her shoes and mouth "Manolo?"

BELLA
Who the magazine wants you to think reads it Fun, chirpy women with no airs and graces. People who like budget fashion and tear-jerker stories, who'll pop down the pub for a lager and lime and remember to ring their mums to ask how the op went when they get back.

Who really reads it The mums having the op and single parents living on high-rise estates for

whom the magazine is the one bright spot in a week spent struggling up 18 flights with a pushchair because the lift's broken, while stepping over empty-eyed addicts on the way to the shops. They also enjoy looking at happy catalogue fashions that they can't afford, and reading about dismal people who've had spooky experiences.

How to impress her Say: "My Nan reads tarot cards – she tells me you're on the up, and a man called Alf is saying not to worry. Listen, let's go down the bingo: there's karaoke on later and we'll have chicken in a basket – I had a win on the horses!" Then wink at her in a devil-may-care fashion.

FRANK
Who the magazine wants you to think reads it Serious, beautiful women working in top jobs and with degrees in politics, women who can discuss Bosnia intelligently over dinner with friends while laughing gently over the growing tendency for post-modernism to be purely self-referential, and the inherent irony therein. They seldom read magazines, but when they do, they expect nothing less than a stimulant for intelligent, well-reasoned debate... and pictures of shoes.

Who really reads it The women who work on it. Their mums. Their cleaners. And anyone who accidentally comes across it in a dentist's waiting room, some years hence.

How to impress her Say: "It's the first magazine that treats a

woman as a whole entity rather than as some addled, fashion-obsessed idiot. And the pictures are amazing! How long have you worked there? Do you want to come for a drink at The Met Bar, I bet they all know you there, don't they? Do you think there'll ever be peace in the Middle East, then?"

THE LADY
Who the magazine wants you to think reads it Gentlewomen of the aristocracy, who rely on its stalwart good sense and taste to provide them with all their domestic staff requirements while lightly diverting them with articles about pressed flowers and the ancient byways of Hampshire.

Who really reads it Snobbish grans who live in sheltered housing, who deliberately leave it on the coffee table so that their next-door neighbour will think she's titled. Self-centred millionaires in Golders Green who want nannies for the children so they can go to Miami for six months. Not to mention aspiring nannies and home-helps who dream of working for Fergie one day and taking Beatrice and Eugenie to the Cheltenham Gold Cup.

How to impress her Assuming she's not a gran or a millionaire, say: "I love children, and I think Louise Woodward was framed. I've got all the celebratory part-works on Diana – have you?" Then dress like James Hewitt on your date.

THE SECRET LIFE OF THE BULLY

What happened to the thyroidal cretins who made your every schoolday a misery?

Douglas's Civil Service bursary came with a price

Your early years were likely plagued by bullies, but now you're an adult, all your troubles tend to come from bespectacled men in middle management roles. So where did all the playground nutters go? Did Bully simply peak too young?

PLAYGROUP Bully was just starting to come into his own. Sporting a primary-coloured dungaree, the short-haired lout would whack anyone who dared enter his torture den – a Wendy House. He'd also be growing big and strong from all that milk he nicked off the others.
His arsenal *Big plastic hammers from a Fisher Price toolkit.*
Counter-measures *You could always tell your mum.*

FIRST SCHOOL With a reputation brought with him from nursery, Bully now had to consolidate his position. Anyone fat, short, ginger or thin was pinned down in the sandpit by his sidekicks and given some "winders" in the guts.
His arsenal *Fists, the ruler and the Clarks polyveldt shoe.*
Counter-measures *Run, or get him in a head-lock and keep him there until break's over.*

MIDDLE SCHOOL Despite his flat-top or skinhead crop, Bully faced his first real competition from nuts from neighbouring schools. Although a couple of defeats are inevitable at this weight, Bully would be putting the finishing touches to his henchman recruitment campaign.
His arsenal *Those trig/compass sets no one knew how to use.*
Counter-measures *Flee, or stay in the library during lunch.*

HIGH SCHOOL Glory days for Bully. His reputation established, bookworms preoccupied with a "future" and initial contact with glue, the school nutter had it sussed. Aggro could be centred around victims' sexual inexperience or the fact that they didn't throw chalk at the duffer who took you for history. These are the days.
His arsenal *Sexual prowess, Class-C drug abuse, and a cold, hard, fear of life "outside".*
Counter-measures *Roll with the punches; await his expulsion.*

FIRST JOB The ground beneath Bully's Docs has started to crumble, with sixth form being for "poofs" only. But with weekends spent helping out his brother on the car lot and the occasional bit of petty crime, Bully could still have fun. "Hey! I'm the man!" he instructs the mirror in his shite car.
His arsenal *Beer bottles and fists.*
Counter-measures *Just go to a decent club of an evening.*

THE KID Bully's got a family now, and his fights are one-sided affairs where his woman gives him a clip. Scared shitless of success stories, he actually smiles when he sees you in the street.
His arsenal *The sympathy card.*
Counter-measures *Blank him as he serves you at the mini-mart.*

THE END This hollow husk, embittered by life, has finally lashed out his tattooed arm at his boss, his wife or his kid. Now he resorts to any work which will see a little dosh in his pocket, so he can piss it away on a horse on a one-way canter to Bostik. This man is no more. You don't look so clever now, do you? Maggot!
His arsenal *Exhausted...*
Counter-measures *Point and laugh when you see him pushing his road sweeper in the early hours.*

Look after your pearlies

Y ou're only given one set of them... well no, you're actually given two, but your full set of adult gnashers should be treated with great care. Left alone, your teeth will go yellow, then green and finally black before falling out. Your breath will stink and nobody will love you. So follow these basic steps and avoid becoming an oral pariah.

■ **Go to your dentist regularly** Don't be afraid of the dentist – the more visits you make, the less terrifying the thought of the drill-master will become. You should go every six months for a clean and a check-up. Always ask if there are any new developments in the field: it's one area of medicine where improvements are continually being made.

■ **Brush carefully** While it is good to brush regularly, don't be over-zealous: you might damage your gums. If they bleed or feel a bit dodgy, get a gum treatment and use it regularly. A very good treatment for gum-

damage is corsodyl – and it'll keep breath fresh.

■ **Use a medical mouth-rinse** A good tool for healthy teeth is Flourigard: rinse out your mouth once a day to avoid dental decay and gum disease. Brits don't use rinses as much as our American cousins – Yanks think our teeth are rotten.

■ **Floss** Real men *do* floss. There's no other way to get bits of beef, toffee and other sticky foodstuffs from between your teeth. Do it gently, once a day, with a flat tape-style floss.

■ **Brush every day** Amazingly, 20% of Britain's population don't brush their teeth every day. Although Scotland makes up most of this percentage, ensure you brush after every meal using a good toothpaste and a

medium-bristled brush. Brush the sides and back of your teeth, not just the ones upfront.

■ **Blitz your own teeth** Tea, coffee and red wine can stain tooth enamel, so try a baking soda-based toothpaste. There are also the new peroxide pastes – the most popular in the US – which have just been given the go-ahead by the British Dental Association.

MacGowan opted for the soup

LIFE IMPROVING TIPS

Don't panic!

P eople get lost. It's a fact. If you find yourself confused in London's Theatreland, simply ask any peeler the way and he'll set you right with a smile and a friendly bit of British banter. Abroad, however, things aren't so easy-going. Thousands of Brits visit Florida every year. Some of them will get lost. If you get marooned in swamp-land, you'll need our guide...

■ **Southern Comfort country** Down in the Everglades, nature and the inbred are the law – there are no happy coppers to help you out. Get caught out here and you're going to need your wits about you. There are no distinguishing landmarks – it's all green and blue-grey. So how do you make it back home?

■ **Watch the current** The landscape will be littered with

creeks, so remember this basic tracking trick: the current generally flows westward, which helps your orientation.

■ **Eat small animals** There will be many edible water rats and small worms. If you're really squeamish, cook 'em; if not, neck 'em whole. Vegetarians will have to risk eating berries, but beware – some are deadly, and many are emetics. Vegans had better take a packed lunch.

■ **Take a gun** Don't try to kill a 'gator with a knife unless you fancy losing an arm. If you shoot one (illegally!) they do taste quite good. Avoid the digestive tract: it tastes bitter and will make you sick. The tail is the best bit – chunky and meaty.

■ **Avoid swamp-dwellers** People that live "out in the

After the accident, Cletus only got to carry a stick

shallow water" are usually unable to fit in with civilised society. They dislike strangers and won't be impressed with your city ways. You could find yourself squealing like a pig if they get hold of you.

■ **Drink rainwater** Fresh water is hard to find in the brackish swamp. Rely on the rain and dew to be found gathered in leaves.

■ **Don't go swimming** Aside from alligators, beware the evil water moccasin: this vicious snake's venom will kill you in six hours if unchecked. And leeches will hook onto your goolies and suck them dry.

■ **Light a fire** It'll warm you up and keep animals away. But the smoke might attract the locals...

ANAL INTRUDERS

The rectum is surely the most versatile of orifices – it seems there's no object that can't find its way up there. But all too often it seems that bottle, hair-dryer or WWII artillery shell has only booked a one-way passage...

NYONE WHO'S GOT DRUNK WITH a medic has heard the story about how they once had to remove a vibrator from the arse of a red-faced patient. But it's not just conventional sex toys that inexplicably get rammed up people's anuses – one US paramedic still dines out on the story of the bloke who inserted a frozen fish into his ring, only for it to thaw out so quickly that its dorsal fin extended, wedging it firmly inside. Here are some other recently reported instances of foreign objects found up mens' butts...

1 When doctors finally managed to remove a sizeable pepper pot from the rectum of their patient, they noticed the inscription "A Present From Marget" on the side. They didn't ask whether Marget had delivered her unique gift by hand.

2 When abrasions around a man's anus were found to have been caused by the blade of a six-inch long screwdriver, he refused to admit he had been playing sexual games. Instead he told doctors that, before taking a shower, he'd sat on a chair in the bathroom and the screwdriver had become lodged up his arse by accident.

Shampoo bottles: common

3 Of the various different types of containers inserted into the anus, shampoo bottles are the most common. Inevitably, when the "victim" presents himself at the hospital, he tells the doctor he slipped in the shower and fell on it.

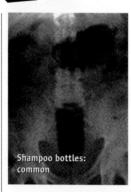

Cigar cases: internal

4 An Alicante man had obviously either run out of matches or got bored of smoking. So to relieve the tedium, he grabbed a metal cigar case and thrust it up himself.

5 A 39-year-old lawyer claimed he'd inserted perfume bottles up his arse on many occasions until finally being unable to remove one. He had tried to extract the bottle of fragrance using a back-scratcher, but to no avail. Doctors eventually administered a spinal anaesthetic before removing the bottle by hand.

6 Whatever patients in A&E might say, objects are rarely inserted into the rectum for non-sexual reasons. But an apparently genuine excuse was given by one Second World War veteran when he presented himself at an East End hospital in the early Nineties. The man had been suffering from a nasty case of haemorroids and, when one particularly unsightly pile hung down into his underpants, he would push it back up using an artillery shell he'd forgotten to hand back in from his days in the Armed Forces. Unfortunately, on this occasion, the shell had become wedged as well.

Shells: wedged

He said he'd no idea what the object was and was amazed at the X-rays

7 When one 25-year-old man got to Casualty, his carefully prepared story went as follows: he visited to a bar, met

PSC

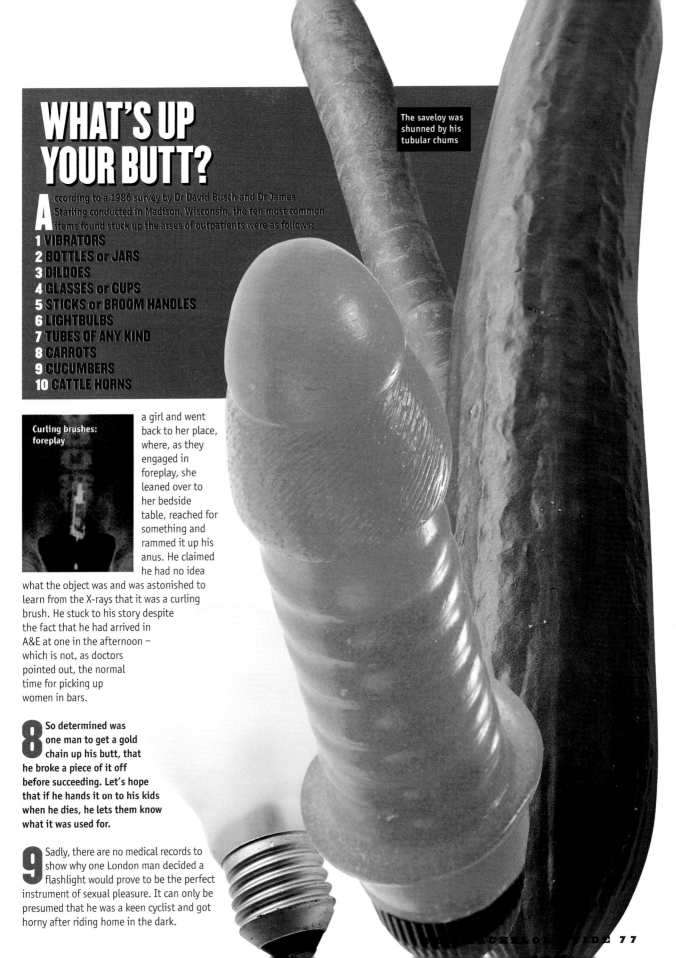

WHAT'S UP YOUR BUTT?

According to a 1986 survey by Dr David Busch and Dr James Starling conducted in Madison, Wisconsin, the ten most common items found stuck up the arses of outpatients were as follows:

1 **VIBRATORS**
2 **BOTTLES or JARS**
3 **DILDOES**
4 **GLASSES or CUPS**
5 **STICKS or BROOM HANDLES**
6 **LIGHTBULBS**
7 **TUBES OF ANY KIND**
8 **CARROTS**
9 **CUCUMBERS**
10 **CATTLE HORNS**

The saveloy was shunned by his tubular chums

Curling brushes: foreplay

a girl and went back to her place, where, as they engaged in foreplay, she leaned over to her bedside table, reached for something and rammed it up his anus. He claimed he had no idea what the object was and was astonished to learn from the X-rays that it was a curling brush. He stuck to his story despite the fact that he had arrived in A&E at one in the afternoon – which is not, as doctors pointed out, the normal time for picking up women in bars.

8 So determined was one man to get a gold chain up his butt, that he broke a piece of it off before succeeding. Let's hope that if he hands it on to his kids when he dies, he lets them know what it was used for.

9 Sadly, there are no medical records to show why one London man decided a flashlight would prove to be the perfect instrument of sexual pleasure. It can only be presumed that he was a keen cyclist and got horny after riding home in the dark.

THE GENT'S

These are the timeless fashion successes that'll make sure you're always in style

Church's black leather brogue, £60

The black leather brogue is the true ambassador for the stylish Brit, having never suffered shifts in footwear fashion like the loafer, DM and square-toe. It's incredibly comfortable and lends itself to any occasion – whether it be formal or casual. That said, the cherry-red version goes best with denim.
STOCKISTS 0800 163519

Levi's indigo 501, £55

Whether it's boot-cut, workwear or clinchback, the denim jean is a wardrobe hardy perennial. But there's nothing that dates quicker, either – see drainpipe, faded and flare – so for all the various styles it's the dark-blue loose-fit you should depend on. Deep pockets, wide bottoms and a dark indigo wash will go with both formal shirt and T.
STOCKISTS 01604 790436

Carhartt woollen beanie hat, £12

With 70 per cent of your body-heat escaping through your head, the humble woollen hat is just as important as your winter coat. And having successfully wriggled free of "home boy" connotations, it can now be worn without the risk of being pulled inside a police car for "questioning".
STOCKISTS 0171-379 4165

Clarks tan suede desert boot, £40

The height of fashion on the scooter footboards of the Sixties Mod, the desert boot is light, suede, sports only a couple of lace-holes and is therefore perfect for summer. Although celebrities like Liam Gallagher, Paul Weller and Richard Ashcroft have elevated its appeal, it's never actually been "out".
STOCKISTS 0990 785 886

Gap grey T-shirt, £10

If asked to name the classic shade of T, most people would say black or white. But the colour to choose, if you can have only one, should really be grey. A shade that likes to be seen with either blue or green – or any other colour you can name – grey is nowhere near as limiting as white and black, and looks just as good under a sweater as it does on its own.
STOCKISTS 0800 427789

DRESSER

Marks & Spencer charcoal lambswool V-neck sweater, £30

Unlike the crew-neck, the classic V can worn over shirt and polo collars as well as the T-shirt. Dark grey suits most colour co-ordinations, and lambswool is neither to thick for summer nor too thin for winter. With fashioned sleeves and a bargain price, this sweater is King Knit.
STOCKISTS 0171-935 4422

Lacoste navy blue polo shirt, £60

It may be pricey, but this perpetually cool item will keep its colour, shape and chic forever. Despite the polo shirt potentially suffering from overkill, the cheeky croc of Lacoste is always a welcome sight. Available in every colour under the sun, this 50-year-old style stalwart is Lord of the Polo.
STOCKISTS 01706 626400

Next cotton flat-fronted trousers, £30

The pleat has suffered awfully recently, and is unlikely to make a comeback for many years to come. These lightweight, flat-fronted strides from Next are a smart alternative to heavy denim or wintery moleskin, and come at a wallet-friendly price. This light brown pair will last you for years and years.
STOCKISTS 01162 849424

Gap Oxford-style white cotton shirt, £30

Oh, the classic white shirt, pulled from the grasp of riff-raff by the dawn of the check and acid-bright. What was considered one of the more low-rent options during the late Eighties/early Nineties is now a wise choice, whether sported beneath a V-neck tank-top or loose on its own over a pair of jeans.
STOCKISTS 0800 427789

Jigsaw Menswear double-breasted knee-length coat, £400

A favourite of James Dean, this classic Fifties-style woollen coat is perfect both for the office and the street. And its length covers a multitude of sins – be they health- or style-related. You could easily get a good 30 years of use out of this winning wardrobe inhabitant.
STOCKISTS 0171-240 5651

RULES OF STYLE WITH DIGBY CRESCENT

Listen and learn as Digby wades through your queries...

Dear FHM,
I bat at number three for my local cricket team. When our opener – and captain – top-edged it to the wickie one sunny day, I started off from the pavilion. As was customary, Skip handed me his cap – but as I continued to the crease I noticed a wriggling critter in his headwear. My problem is two-fold: was I right to have removed what was obviously a head-louse from the cap and wear it as if nothing was wrong (which I did); and secondly, should I tell my captain that he has an embarrassing infestation – which would be an obvious risk to my place in the team?

Truly, you are between a rock and a hard place. The moment to broach the subject with your captain may arise in the course of locker-room banter, but in the meantime – buy your own cap.

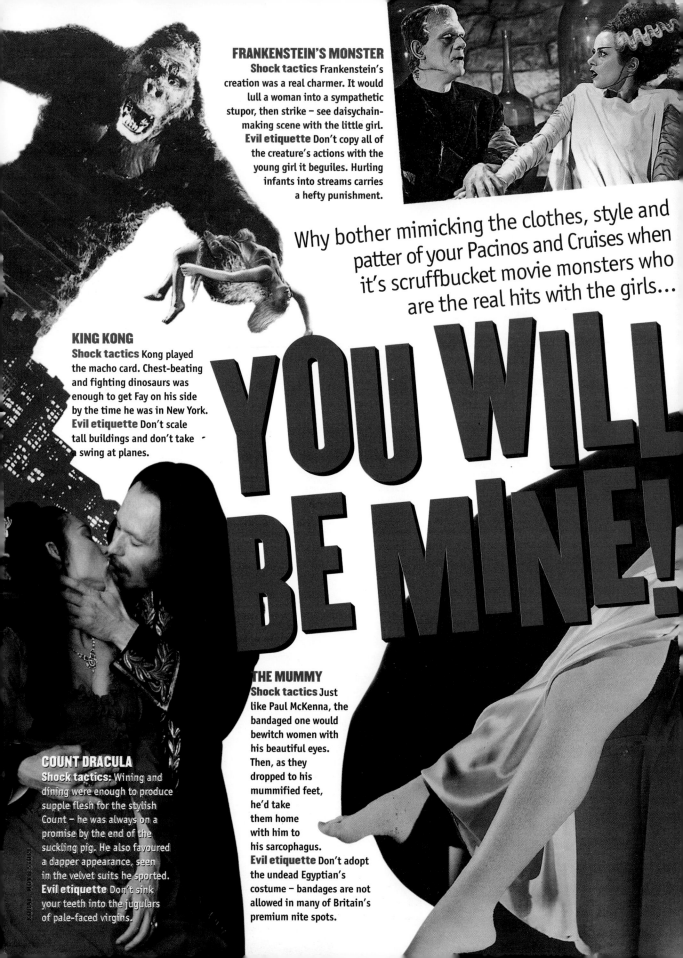

FRANKENSTEIN'S MONSTER
Shock tactics Frankenstein's creation was a real charmer. It would lull a woman into a sympathetic stupor, then strike – see daisychain-making scene with the little girl. **Evil etiquette** Don't copy all of the creature's actions with the young girl it beguiles. Hurling infants into streams carries a hefty punishment.

Why bother mimicking the clothes, style and patter of your Pacinos and Cruises when it's scruffbucket movie monsters who are the real hits with the girls...

YOU WILL BE MINE!

KING KONG
Shock tactics Kong played the macho card. Chest-beating and fighting dinosaurs was enough to get Fay on his side by the time he was in New York. **Evil etiquette** Don't scale tall buildings and don't take a swing at planes.

COUNT DRACULA
Shock tactics: Wining and dining were enough to produce supple flesh for the stylish Count – he was always on a promise by the end of the suckling pig. He also favoured a dapper appearance, seen in the velvet suits he sported. **Evil etiquette** Don't sink your teeth into the jugulars of pale-faced virgins.

THE MUMMY
Shock tactics Just like Paul McKenna, the bandaged one would bewitch women with his beautiful eyes. Then, as they dropped to his mummified feet, he'd take them home with him to his sarcophagus. **Evil etiquette** Don't adopt the undead Egyptian's costume – bandages are not allowed in many of Britain's premium nite spots.

FREDDIE KREUGER

Shock tactics Freddie favoured the use of entering into teenage girls' dreams. Difficult. However, mention to your prey that she's been in yours.
Evil etiquette Avoid slicing 'n' dicing her with finger-based razors. At least on the first date.

THE WEREWOLF

Shock tactics Another exploiter of the sympathy vote, the wolfman would tell women that only their love could break his eternal curse. Cried a lot as well.
Evil etiquette Don't howl at the sky on a full moon or rip haunches off deer with your teeth. This tends to offend.

QUASIMODO

Shock tactics Quasi bagged a beauty by overexaggerating his thanks for a glass of water.
Evil etiquette Don't hole yourself up in a bell tower – these are only frequented by bespectacled "ringers".

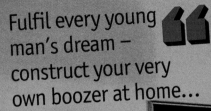

Fulfil every young man's dream – construct your very own boozer at home…

"DRINK UP &

Re-decorate the room
■ Attach to the wall that set of gold discs that The Wurzels accidentally left in your real local one boozy night four years ago.
■ Mount a photograph of the Queen Mother trying to pour a pint of bitter on the wall above the fireplace.
■ Flock wallpaper is a must.

Re-arrange your furniture
■ Take some stools from the breakfast bar and place around the nested tables in the living room.
■ Remember to close the gap between the table nearest to the bar and the bar itself so that drinkers will have to squeeze through, spilling other people's pints and prompting scenes of ugly, mindless violence.
■ Make sure one table is located next to the very draughtiest doorway.
■ Fix a rotating propeller fan on the ceiling, taking care to make it really wobbly and likely to crash to the floor.

Acquire some receptacles
■ "Borrow" some glasses, beer mats and beer towels from your local. Your dad may even let you borrow his pewter tankard or Toby Jug for your grand opening.
■ Don't forget the ladies. Make sure you have a couple of half-pint glasses to hand, ensuring that both have some of your old dear's lipstick already smeared around the rim.

The pool table
■ The centrepiece of any boozer. First, make sure the coin-operated slot is a) overpriced – £1.60 should suffice – and b) defective.
■ All cushions should have as much life in them as a wet night in Bangor.
■ There should be five or six cues in the rack, but only one with a tip suitable for playing with. Obviously, that particular cue must be too short for most adults to use and should be as bent as a U-bend.
■ Last but not least, remove any sign of chalk from the premises.

Prepare some pub grub
■ Ignore classier, more expensive brands of crisps in favour of low-rent products like Tavern Snacks.
■ For that authentic feel, place a complimentary bowl of peanuts on the bar for your mates to dip their fingers in after going for a piss.
■ Only offer "home-cooked" food if you live within five minutes of a chippy or curry house. That way, you can slip out the back door and return laden with cod and chips or lamb dhansak. Don't forget the hefty mark-up on what you paid for them!

ELIZABETH WHITING ASSOCIATES

F***K OFF MUM!"

Behind the bar
■ Position amusing placards with hilarious advice such as: "Please don't ask for credit, as a punch in the mouth often offends."
■ Take an A3 poster of Suzanne Mizzi and staple some packets of peanuts to it, so that, as demand increases, the prospect of a glimpse of nipple becomes a very real possibility.
■ Forge some postcards sent by your regulars while on their holidays.
■ Manufacture your own range of pub merchandise that nobody in their right mind will ever buy.

Assemble a bar area
■ Clear your living room and cover the carpet in a pre-prepared sugar solution, so your feet will stick to it.
■ Paint the walls and ceiling a murky shade of yellow to give the impression of years of nicotine abuse.
■ Hang a bell over a trestle table bar for those last orders demands.

Offer a range of traditional pub entertainment
■ Attach a dartboard to the wall and a shove ha'penny table in a patently unsuitable location. And of course, those pictures of dogs smoking and playing pool are obligatory.
■ Make sure there are dominoes and a beer-soaked pack of cards for the older punter. Anyone caught playing Jenga should be barred instantly.
■ Get a wall bracket for your TV and tune it so that the picture is barely discernible. Ensure only a couple of chairs offer any semblance of a view.

Pub miscellany
■ Employ a dog to sit under the table with its own ashtray of warm bitter to lap at of an evening.
■ Have your little brother collect empties in return for a bag of ready salted crisps and a small glass of coke for an entire shift's work.
■ Learn the appropriate jargon for last orders. ("Haven't you got homes to go to?", "Will you please be drinking up?", "Is that dead?" and "Get the fuck out of my house, you pissed-up little prick!")

On the door
Draw a picture of man wearing a leather blouson with outdated flares on the outside of the door. Then add a felt-tip "comedy" cock and balls, as if scribbled on by a drunken student.

The urinals
Insert useless blue toilet "fresheners" for the authentic pub bog feel, and, obviously, remove all signs of cleaning. Jam the cisterns with fag ends, then vomit in a couple of them.

Above the urinals
Daub selected graffiti on the walls (e.g. Anarchy symbols, "ring Kaz on 555432 for a good time", "Pompey Boyz on Tour", etc.).

The towel rail
Take three filthy towels. Wash for several weeks mixed with items of clothing guaranteed to run: indigo jeans and black Rancid T-shirts give best results. Stitch together in a loop. Hang.

The window
Remove all fittings, thereby guaranteeing that the window will never close properly. Rest assured, the resultant icy gale will in no way remove the bitter tang of urine festering in the air.

The walls
To create that authentic Bobby Sands environment, smear your khazi's walls with brown boot polish or HP Sauce to generate a full set of dubious stains.

The floor
Drench the tiles with great lakes of piss. If the idea of urinating on your own floor appals you, use those eight unwanted cans of Norseman lager Uncle Terry brought round last Christmas.

The sink
Disconnect the hot water tap, while ensuring that even the slightest feathering of the cold fawcet results in a Niagaran torrent of freezing, trouser-drenching embarassment.

NOW WASH YOUR HANDS....

Complement a living-room boozer with your own pub toilet

HOW TO TAIL AN AUTOMOBILE
Driver, follow that car!

Buzzing learner drivers gave Edmunds the horn

Okay. There may not be many times in your life when you find it necessary to tail a car. But consider this scenario: your girl comes out of the local hop with another guy. They get into his Datsun 280z with mag wheels, burn rubber and leave you weeping in the dust. Had you followed our advice you could have tailed the cheap bint, then given her and laughing boy a piece of your mind.

■ **Go for an engine that rocks** Your own motor is the place to start in any chase. If your car is bogus, you'll lose your quarry. Make sure you have a full tank and are ready to go, and that your car isn't too distinctive. Blending in is essential, but make sure you don't go overboard in the disguise stakes: a dog-shaped car à la *Dumb And Dumber* will draw attention. The FBI always use blue or grey sedans.

■ **Don't be gung-ho with your driving** This will piss other motorists off and make you stand out. It's a good idea to remain a few vehicles behind the one you are tailing. If you do go mad and mount pavements, speed, etc, the chances are you'll be pulled over by the police anyway.

■ **Avoid passing your quarry** You shouldn't pass the car you are following as this may lead to some tricky manoeuvring – and let's face it, it's missing the point a bit, isn't it.

■ **Pay attention to how the other driver is driving** Problems will occur if the other driver suspects that he is being followed. He will normally slow down, then speed up a few times, take obscure corners and may even pull in. If this behaviour starts, you've been rumbled, and might as well give up the chase.

■ **Be prepared for a nighttime chase** There is no way of telling how long a pursuit will last, so try to get to the target car before the trail starts. You could try taping over one of his brake lights: this will make his motor stand out at night, even if he gets several cars ahead of you.

HOW TO HANG A SHELF
"Don't buy one..."

Blokes do DIY. It's the law. However, if, like most of us, the only practical building work you've done was with lettered wooden cubes as a child, you may need some pointers. One of the most basic DIY jobs on Earth is putting up shelves. Using our tips, you should end up with a set of level beauties on which to store all those books you mean to read.

■ **Mark the height of the shelf** Make sure you leave enough space between shelves for what you are going to put on them. Mark out the lines in pencil, using a spirit level. Don't think you'll get away with doing it by eye: as soon as you turn in the last screw you'll notice that your shiny new shelf is what builders refer to as "pissed".

■ **Use wooden supports** Cut wooden support battens to suit the depth of the shelves. If you want something a little more stylish, try cutting the front ends of the supports to a 45-degree angle.

■ **Watch out for sagging** This occurs when the span of the shelves is too long in relation to the thickness of the wood you are using. To avoid sagging, solid timber or blockboard (with its core running lengthways) is excellent. Veneered chipboard, although popular because of its low cost, will eventually snag and break. If you do use chipboard, make sure you take the precaution of adding in supports at regular intervals.

■ **Use good screws** Once you have drilled your holes in the wall, put in rawlplugs that are the right size for the screws. If you make the holes too big, or use loose rawlplugs, the supports will simply pull everything out the moment you load your gear on to the shelves. And that's no bloody good, is it?

○ **Without his team, Wilf Lunn was hopeless**

LIFE IMPROVING TIPS

THE WEST RESIDENCE

CHAIN-FREE – OWNER MUST SELL

0192 567 893

ARE YOU BUYING A KILLER'S DEN?

It seems only yesterday that Fred and Rosemary West's innocuous abode was revealed as a nest of death. How do you tell if your des res has ever been used by killers with a little more nous than the gruesome pair from Gloucester? Here's the *FHM* survey of a psycho killer's lair...

THE FRONT GARDEN The first giveaway to a murderer's one-time retreat is the well-tendered front lawn. Of course, this doesn't mean that every blue-rinsed pensioner and her cardiganed hubby are potential killers, but it does look a bit odd if the garden out back, by contrast, is an unkempt mess. The front lawn is the surburban psycho's way of saying: "Look – nothing odd about this house. I've done me gardening."

THE FRONT DOOR A killer doesn't want snoopers grabbing a glimpse of his or her activities, so you'll find no lattice-crossed or stained-glass windows. Oh no. You're much more likely to find a sturdy, solid entrance with no potential for glass breakages resulting from a captive's desperate escape. Be wary of a highly-sprung slit of a letterbox: these are sure indicators of ungodly activities within.

THE WINDOWS The front room's windows will either have blinds pulled down or feature a thick curtain, and may be double-glazed for soundproofing. Check for claw-marks on inside sills. And frosted glass in a front room is the latest in nouveau serial killer chic.

THE HALL The hall will likely be wide and uncluttered, as many cadavers will have to be hauled through it on their journey to the garden or downstairs to the cellar. A wooden floor is the perfect wipe-free, smooth surface, whereas a carpet would provide unwanted friction, implant fibres into the body and can be a bugger to clean.

THE FRONT ROOM Although most of the action actually takes place elsewhere, a lot of the hideous planning goes on right here. Victims may be lured into a false sense of security in this rather pleasant place. Why, then, the plastic-covered suite the previous

FHM ESTATES

DAHMER ACRES

INCLUDES SPACIOUS BASEMENT

0192 567 893

REX

UNABOMBER HUT

HANDY FOR COURTS, INSANITY HEARINGS, ETC.

0192 567 893

(good for burials), a small furnace for disposal of carcasses and their possesions, and hooks and rings on the beams of the floorboards above for suspending victims. There may also be an open sack of builder's lime: this is used to quench the odours of the dead. And if there is no cellar in your potential property, check the loft. Carefully.

THE FRONT BEDROOM To the untrained eye, it looks like a typical suburban bedroom: perhaps a bay window looks out over a leafy street. But check for peepholes drilled into the wall joining it to the single room at the back of the house. These are clearly for observation and pre-kill pleasures.

THE BACK BEDROOM Why, you'll ask yourself, should such a little room have a heavy-duty mortice lock on its peculiarly heavy oak door? This, my friend, is to keep the killer's quarry in, and prying eyes out. True bloodlust is let loose when the terror of the back room is unleashed. You can usually cut the stifling death-niff with a cheesewire.

THE BATHROOM There'll be a bath, toilet and sink, just like a normal bathroom, but even an arsenal of industrial-strength cleaning gear will have failed to erase the stains from the porcelain sink and bath combo. The tiles, too, will have clotted muck in their grouting. Check behind pipes and in cisterns for a killer's makeshift tools.

THE GARDENS After the pleasure of the front lawn, the back garden will scream at you: "Abandon all hope, those who enter here." There will be a lot of inexplicable things: a cement mixer; small heaps of freshly-turned soil; a huge shovel; an enormous bonfire patch. Strange plastic bag-like protrusions peak up through the unmowed grass and flap in the wind, and the shrubs seem overly healthy, as if on a contant drip of Baby Bio.

owner left behind? And expect to find radiators and electric three-bars for heating – any busy serial killer won't have been wasting precious time pottering about with firelighters and coal.

THE KITCHEN/DINER Usually you'll find a hatch connecting this room with the front room: our evil tenants will have left their victims alone, then spied on them as they made "a nice cup of tea". The floor is most likely easywipe lino. And keep an eye open for raised, cracked damp spots *en route* to the back door, plus any gouging, kick-marks or embedded fingernails in the door-jamb.

THE CELLAR You should know what to look out for in any cellar of ill repute. Forget about old clothes and yellowing newspapers; in a true death house you'll find a dirt floor

"IT'S NOT QUITE WHAT WE HAD IN MIND"

Any one of the following danger signs should have you scrambing for the front door...

Plasterboard walls
A simple rap with your knuckles should reveal a good, solid wall. If not, the cavity space could be a Pandora's box of limbs, weapons and frantically scrawled messages of help scatched into bare brick.

Strange bits and pieces
Any unexplained stains should trigger alarm bells: a bottle of red wine wouldn't create a matted brown patch 14in by 16in, so what would? And if the plugholes are blocked with any of the following, it's time to leave: a coagulated mess of blood and

hair; small bones and teeth; fingernails.

Unwanted garden pests
Every garden attracts the occasional bluebottle and bumble bee, but a swarm of flies suggests decay and foul blood. Another danger sign is the posse of fat neighbourhood cats, plump from the rancid titbits dug up in the back yard.

Overstocked cleaning cupboards
Previous tenants often leave a tin of Vim and a few J-Cloths nestling amid the plumbing, but cracked spectacles, hacksaws and burgundy-stained rubber

gloves are not normal under-sink fare.

Literature
Well-thumbed, annotated copies of *Catcher In The Rye* – the staple read of killer hippie Charlie Manson and Lennon assassin Mark Chapman – and books concerning the occult and witchcraft are a real giveaway.

Shoeboxes
A Clarks shoebox full of jewellery, unused train tickets, passport photos and loose coins would be a typical collection of memories – but of how many people? This is a trophy of lost souls, for sure.

ARE YOU EVIL?

If you can get the voices in your head to belt up for a minute, take this serial killer test – in handy multiple-choice format!

1 You come home after a hard day's work to find your dog at the door with one of your trainers stuffed into its trap. What do you do?
a) Let out a laboured tut, wag your finger at the dewey-eyed mischief-maker, and forgive it.
b) Wrestle the shoe from the dog's mouth and send him to his basket.
c) Pick him up by the neck and march him to the cellar, where you dip the foul, filthy beast into a vat of bubbling acid.

2 You wake in the middle of the night, to find your partner dead to the world. What do you think?
a) "Aah, look at my little baby, all fast asleep," as you stare at the object of your dreams.
b) "If it wasn't for your snoring, I'd be asleep too. Never mind..."
c) "Oh yes, my pretty one – you've done it now, you whore!" Then reach for the gleaming blade you've hidden in her pyjama case.

3 You're feeling a little lonely, so you invite a few friends round for dinner. You've had a wonderful time, but now it's time for them to leave. What do you do?
a) Slap them on the back, arrange a night out for the following week and see them to the door.
b) Engage in a heart-to-heart with your closest pal, and maybe sit into the early hours sharing a bottle of single malt.
c) Give your friends a poisoned night-cap, engage in necrophilic sex, then position the cadavers around the dinner table until they start to decompose.

4 Your boss has been giving you a hard time at work. What do you do?
a) Try a little harder at your job to prove him wrong.
b) Have it out with him or her and tell them to get stuffed.
c) Follow your boss home, enter his or her house, dispose of their partner and hide under the duvet clutching an ice pick.

5 Your girfriend's left you for someone else, but says you can keep the house. How do you feel?
a) Depressed for a few months, but then, when you're ready, you look for someone more suitable.
b) Get very bitter, drink a lot, and use the house as a shagging den.
c) Plaster the walls with her likeness, photograph her and her new lover and send threats made from cut-up newspapers and voice-synthesised phone calls every hour on the hour.

6 You're looking after a flat for a friend, who says you can help yourself to whatever's in the fridge. What do you do?
a) Think "what a nice gesture", but buy your own food anyway.
b) Shout "Oh, yes!", then gorge on everything they have.
c) Think: "Sod the cod steaks!" Then gouge out the throat of their moggy before sporting the severed head as a bracelet.

7 On the way home from a Christmas party, a beggar asks you for a little change. What do you do?
a) Fumble for some cash and wish him a happy Yuletide.
b) Walk on by without making eye contact, mumbling something like, "No change, mate."
c) Drag the maggot to the nearest skip and pull his sunken eyes from their sockets as his screams disappear into the night.

8 Sitting at home, bored, you try to find something to amuse yourself with. What do you do?
a) Pop down to Blockbuster and rent one of their latest releases.
b) Get wrestless, slip off to the pub and get rat-arsed.
c) Take matches and a can of paraffin and torch the house opposite.

9 Old age has taken your mother from you, and you're obviously upset. What do you do?
a) Arrange a nice funeral and construct a loving ode to the "best mother in the world".
b) Get a bit depressed, and take it out on the bottle for a few weeks.
c) Steal her cadaver from the morgue and dance around it wearing her clothes to reincarnate her spirit.

RATINGS

■ Mostly "a"s: you're perfectly normal. Maybe too normal. Try livening up a little and throw caution to the wind every now and again.
■ Mostly "b"s: you're a little fiery, though you never go over the top. But sometimes a little patience can usurp aggression.
■ Mostly "c"s: sweet screaming Jesus, you're a monster!

10 The council comes to lay new water pipes in your garden. What do you do?
a) Usher them through – after all, the old ones had been leaking.
b) Wait impatiently while they fiddle about in the garden.
c) Jump onto the flower beds in a frenzy so as to cover up the people "at rest" below.

RULES OF STYLE WITH DIGBY CRESCENT

Listen and learn as Digby wades through your queries...

Dear FHM,
My mother, recently widowed, has attempted to ease the pain of her loneliness by purchasing a pet – a fluffy angora rabbit. Her friends all coo around the doe-eyed herbivore, but every time I see it, I can think of nothing except stringing it up by its loathsome neck from the washing line. What's the matter with me? Am I sick in the head?

I cannot help but be alarmed by your violent over-reaction to your mother's furry companion. In the short term, I suggest you feign a simple allergy to the hair of the rabbit, which means you won't have to play with the thing when you visit. In the long term, why not turn your violence towards animals to your advantage – a career as a butcher, gamekeeper or shampoo-tester seems cut out for you, my lad.

"Don't make me angry..."

"Oh Chuck, you're right – it's racing!"

You may, like Ghandi and Martin Luther King, think that passive resistance is the best way to put your point across, but just in case you reconsider when someone has a pop, you should learn to defend yourself. And what better defence than attack? Spend a few hours a day shadow-boxing and you should be confident of fending off even the biggest louts. Failing that, you'll at least look noble as you pitch towards the pavement.

■ **Footwork** Not only do you want to be able to dance from an oncoming opponent, but good footwork adds power and speed. Keep your back foot riding slightly on the ball of your toes, while your leading foot (the opposite side to your leading fist) should be pointing forward at an angle.

■ **The left jab** It's vital to keep your right hand at your right cheek, looking to defend, while you use your left to hit your opponent in the face with short, sharp motions. Lisped insults, à la Mike Tyson and Prince Naseem, are inadvisable: they only get your opponent riled.

■ **The straight right** In this case, you're trying for a single, forceful hit. Twist your body and push off your back foot. Remember to put your body-weight behind the punch and "drive through" your man.

■ **"The old one-two"** Now you're connecting shots and beginning to look every bit the pro. Follow the left jab with a straight right. If it feels right, you're doing well, and should start to push forward...

■ **The left hook** This time, drop your left shoulder slightly and, as you punch, twist your body to the right and drive off from your back foot. Your target here is the temple or the jaw.

■ **The uppercut** You need to be very close to your opponent to achieve this. Drop your shoulders and bring your fist up vertically to smash him in the chin. As long as your body-weight is behind the punch, it'll be a success – provided you make contact. Miss, and you're wide open for punishment.

Get your own way

While a smile and an easy manner may win you friends, it won't always get you what you want. Look around you – the people who always get their own way are the whiners and whingers. You can learn from these miserable people: turn off the charm and watch in wonder as you get just what you desire.

■ **Make sure you're a good complainer** If you want to grumble about something, don't hold back. Get stuck straight in as soon as you spot the crack.

Traffic wardens: unimpressed by long words

■ **When arguing, your aim is to win** Know your goals and be sure you achieve them, and strive to make your point. To this end, it helps if you have an ultimate point which you can drive towards.

■ **If you can't win, don't argue...** There's nothing more embarrassing than a public freak-out. If you find yourself drawn into an argument until you're defending a "no win" point – such as "salt is sweet" – then drop out. Don't get more and more fantastic in your claims. You'll still lose.

■ **Be confident** A bit of flannel can go a long way – look at Arthur Daley. Although you don't want to sound too wide, a bit of knowledge delivered in the right way can bring your foe round to your point of view.

■ **Keep eye contact** This will aggravate the person you're throwing your strop at; a glance elsewhere and they will take less notice. It's proven that people are intimidated by an unwavering stare.

■ **Don't be afraid of causing a scene** It's worth it if you are in the right. If, say, you're in a restaurant and your soup really is cold, the last thing the staff want is for you to start yelling about it to all and sundry.

■ **Invent facts to back up your stroppiness** If said with conviction, no one will question them. The more solid you sound as you deliver your argument-winning pack of lies, the better.

■ **Use big words to confuse others** Most people in Britain have a vocabulary of only 600 words. If you get stuck in a corner, simply throw in the occasional impossible-to-identify word and you'll be back on top in no time.

LIFE IMPROVING TIPS

KOBAL, MICK HUTSON

TOILET TRAINING

Don't flush too early – every stool can provide a full medical history

Children and animals love to stare at their bowel offerings – and if we want to keep healthy, we ought to be following suit. Examine the key features of your excreta and turn a movement into a valuable diagnostic tool...

VOLUME The average number of stools produced per week is 9.6 for men and 7.1 for women. "A normal westerner eating a standard diet could expect to produce 100 to 200 millilitres a day," says Dr Tony Coll of Addenbrokes Hospital in Cambridge. If you produce much more than this, it may indicate too much fibre and water in your diet; whereas much less could be a sign of too little. If your daily offering is more accurately measured in litres, you may have an infection in your gut, preventing it from breaking down and absorbing food and intestinal secretions. The volume passed can be up to ten litres a day in some severe cases of infectious diarrhoea: if you go this much, you don't need to be told that you've got a problem.

CONSISTENCY A healthy stool should be a solid, smooth and soft log, passed without straining. "High-fibre diets produce a much softer, bulkier stool than those of a person taking in less fibre,"

"Jenkins Minor's been eating sweetcorn again!"

says Dr Coll. Again, a very soft or hard stool may indicate either too much or too little fibre in the diet, while a stool that is fluid-like with a greasy or oily surface could be a sign that food isn't being properly absorbed in your gut, possibly due to an infection.

COLOUR Faeces gets its colour from bile discharged from the liver, so it follows that a putty-coloured stool is a classic sign of a blockage in the bile duct and might even indicate liver disease. On the other hand, a jet-black, shiny stool could contain partially digested blood, which must have been discharged into your gut from somewhere. And bright red blood could, in extreme

cases, be a sign of bowel cancer, and should be taken seriously. "Certain types of food and medication can also influence colour," says Dr Coll. So if your stool is only slightly redder than usual, it may just be because you've been eating beetroot.

SMELL Your stool's odour is influenced by the amount of protein you eat. "Very high-protein diets can result in a particularly offensive smell," says Dr Coll. If your stool smells like something's crawled up your arse and died, it may be another sign that food isn't being absorbed properly. And if it floats, won't flush away and is pale and gassy, the cause could be colic disease.

KNOW YOUR STOOL

Log-shaped and soft with a smooth surface: A superb, healthy specimen of a stool. You must be doing something right.

Very hard, small lumps: You have what is known as a "slow transit time". It's a fairly safe bet that you're suffering from constipation, either caused by your diet or a problem in your gut, such as an infection.

Strong-smelling, mushy, fluid-like lumps and water: You have a "fast transit time". You're likely suffering from diarrhoea, which, again, could be caused either by something as simple as your diet, or possibly by an underlying problem in your gut.

Bloody: You may have laughed it off as piles for years, and you could be right. But blood in the faeces could also be a sign of bowel cancer, so go see the doc.

KOBAL

ANIMAL LOVE

Why bother with sex advice from bespectacled agony aunts? Take a tip from the beasts – they never go short!

THE TOPI

What's its game? The herbivorous males have two tricks up their cloven sleeves come mating time. The first is a scent emitted from skin glands in order to mark territories and attract mates. The follow-up to the male topi's fine line in fragrances is its horn, which, once evolved for combat, has become a target for sexual selection among the females of the herd. As lady topis go for large horns, "big ones" become increasingly valuable to males, leading to even greater preference by the females.
In practice: You'll need a foul-smelling aftershave and an elasticated horn.

THE BADGER

What's its game? The European badger is a real one-woman man. Not only does it stay with the same bride for its entire life-span, but the stripey weed bows down to his girl's every demand. When the *female* feels horny, she lets the male know by urinating in his face. The male then digs a trough for his old lady to sit in, so that mating can commence. Once she's sitting comfortably, the male badger nips in from behind and, taking as little time as possible, shoots his load.
In practice: Crouch beneath a pissed-up girl at a taxi rank, and offer to be her loo.

THE SHARK

What's its game? Unlike most fish, this evil killing machine fertilises the female's eggs internally, making its mating behaviour more akin to the human's than any other sea-dweller. When a male shark sees a bit of tail he fancies, he goes up to her shoulder and takes a chomp out of it – a little like the "love bite" that decorated our teenage years. The reason for the hot biting action: the male claspers (buck teeth) are used in the process of transferring sperm from the male to the female – so it's actually the good old chomper that rocks girl sharks' worlds.
In practice: This isn't a bad animal to mimic: file down your canines and go for the neckline.

THE CRESTED GREBE

What's its game? As well as having beautiful plumage, this critter is not too shy in coming forward, either. With a beautifully-choreographed mating routine, the male dances – wings a-flappin' – in mid-air for his mistress, who floats beneath him, happily bemused by his actions. Then, if the lady's suitably impressed, she joins in – if only as a brief precursor for sexual intercourse.
In practice: A complicated dance like this will end in tears if you don't do it right. On the other hand, with a little tuition, she's all yours.

THE HIPPOPOTAMUS

What's its game? Due to its considerable girth, the hippo has an alarming accident rate when it comes to sex – with many girl hippos being crushed underneath their enormous suitors. And the pulling procedure is no more sophisticated. Basically, the male hippo rolls around in a pool of mud, spraying his woman with the slop. The lady then falls at his feet, ready for penetration.
In practice: If you get a girl who'll fall for this, you're laughing.

THE PRAYING MANTIS

What's its game? This feeble-minded buffoon is everything to hate in a man. He goes out of his way to attact a lady, fertilises her, then gets eaten for his troubles.
In practice: Forget it.

THE SEA SLUG

What's its game? Being hermaphrodite, this sea-floor dweller has to get it together with its own. Endowed with both male and female external organs, one randy slug must position itself side-by-side with the opposite flank of another, so that the one's penis side is adjacent to the other's vagina. Sperm is then transferred in the usual way, as the two nudibranchs entwine themselves into a "love coil".
In practice: Forgetting your sexuality for a minute, the adoption of the slug's techniques means taking up line-dancing.

THE GIRAFFE

What's its game? It may have an unfeasibly long neck, but that doesn't stop this majestic creature from getting its jollies. In fact, the giraffe has more orgasms than any other living creature. When a male sees a female he fancies, he simply walks over and rubs his neck against hers, thus rendering her weak at the knees. He then engages in a bit of petting, before quickly jumping up top and driving it home.
In practice: This necking ritual is fairly normal for the average human – just don't try it while sporting a rollneck sweater made from itchy, man-made fibres.

FLEECE YOUR FRIENDS!

Spend all your cash on beer, then win it back from your drink-addled mates by turning your living room into a fixed gypsy fairground!

SCORE 11 OR UNDER

This fairground activity is a discipline that only the most skilled arrowsmith can master. But all drunks love darts, and your mates will be gagging for a crack at this three-arrow favourite. You can stack the odds even further in your favour by "loading" your arrows, gypsy-style. Buy a set of the crappy plastic ones like the pikeys use at fairs, then chew the flights, bend the shafts, blunt the points with a file and invisibly harden low-scoring areas of the board by painting them with sugary water, glue or egg white. You'll be quids in.

THE PING-PONG STING

Take a selection of glasses, place them in a tight circle on your coffee table and invite friends to lob ping-pong balls into them. At a quid for three chucks – with a crisp tenner to the victor who actually manages to get one to remain in a vessel – the odds will seem pretty favourable to a drink-befuddled mind. But even if a ball does enter cleanly into the mouth of a glass (which, of course, it won't, because you've selected your narrowest receptacles), it will regularly bounce straight out again. Ker-chingg!

FRONT ROOM BOWLS

Using a lemon as the "jack" and four oranges per man as your "woods", challenge your pals to a round of "nearest to the jack takes a tenner". You will, of course, give them the most ovoid citrus fruits on God's good Earth, which will never roll in a straight line. And make sure you've memorised every subtle nuance of your floorboards/ carpet in advance. Thanks very much.

"And for you, my friend – the quince"

COOKER RING HOOP-LA

Remove the chrome ring surrounds from your electric cooker. Carefully place six full two-litre coke bottles on your coffee table, then, around the central one, hold a shiny tenner in pride of place with a rubber band. Around the rest, write out a variety of mystery forfeits on cards, such as: "You get the first round in tomorrow night"; "Make the teas, you stinking queen"; and "Cough up a fiver, gaylord". Invite your pals in, get their money and let them toss the rings, making sure you retire to bed a richer man. Incidentally, the gap around the central bottle will never be big enough to accept a ring. Everyone's a winner. Well, maybe not everyone.

Señor Martini would often harangue the locals from his Vermouth roadshow

THE WEIGHTED CAMPARI MINIATURES SCAM

This is a living room-based variant on fairground coconut shy and pop gun "target" games. Place five bright-red Campari miniatures on your window sill, having first dropped a small but supremely effective pile of lead fishing shot into each bottle. The violent scarlet colour of the grog will conceal your weighty additions, which means that although your drunken pals will hurl ping-pong balls at them all night long, they'll never budge an inch. Money for old rope.

Oliver Reed loved his ten-pin bowling set

THE VIDEO LIFT

A variant of the Brick Lift, in which Britain's bearded behemoth, Geoff Capes, holds the world record. Big hands and a wide armspan are a huge advantage.

Begin with 15 video cases, with the cassettes still inside. Competitors have to lift the stack like a concertina and hold them together for five seconds to achieve a successful lift. After each round, an extra video case is added to the stack, until a winner emerges. A lift is considered invalid if the cases are not parallel to the surface from which they were lifted.

HEAVE!

Recreate The World's Strongest Man competition in your own home – using nothing but everyday domestic object

PHOTOGRAPHY: MICK HUTSON; STYLING: ISSY VIRDEN; CLOTHES AND TRAINERS: REEBOK

THE SOFA PULL

The trick here – just like the real thing, the Juggernaut Pull – is to get low and adopt the same angle as foolhardy Finnish ski-jumpers when they hurl themselves off the high ramp.

Fasten a rope (or some sheets tied together) to the sofa and round the upper body of the competitor, then time how long it takes the contender to drag the thing across the living room until he can touch the opposite wall.

THE BEER CRATE RELAY

A strength-sapping test of stamina based on the Barrel Relay, designed to test the power of the thighs and arms as well as your speed off the mark. The booze must be consumed once the contest is over.

Take five full crates of beer and place them at the foot of the stairs. Lift the first crate and carry it to the top of the stairs, depositing it on the upstairs landing. Return to the next crate and do the same thing again, until each crate has been transported. The clock stops the moment the final crate lands upstairs. Note that if a competitor attempts to lighten the load by cracking open a bottle mid-event, he is immediately disqualified.

THE TV LIFT

Based on the original Battery Lift, as perfected by American giant Bill Kazmaier, this event offers those with shorter arms a distinct advantage. Remember to check your household insurance beforehand, so as to cover the cost of a replacement TV set in case of breakage.

Taking the TV in both hands and using the legs for power, lift the set until it is at chest height. Hold the TV out until both arms are fully extended, and start timing. Stop the clock as soon as the arms fail to maintain that 90° angle.

HELL-HOLE!

In television adverts, a man's bathroom is an eye-smartingly bright temple to personal hygiene. The reality, of course, is far, far different…

The plughole Invariably full of matted hair, meaning that even a small basin of shaving water takes the best part of a month to empty. Worse, when tugged, the offending collection of hair will keep coming out in the manner of an unsavoury Paul Daniels silk handkerchief trick… except that your "hanky" will have the texture of a slimy Tarzan vine and will smell like a mass grave.

Towels It's a fact: women always smell a man's towels when they use his bathroom for the first time. So it goes without saying that the acrid stench of improperly dried towelling and pongy man-musks will offend – while curious, unidentifiable brown streaks could quite literally kill. Dark-coloured towels are the worst offenders, hiding a multitude of the very worst masculine sins.

The bath The massive expanse of clinkers and mud abandoned by retreating water levels in the average man's bath would humble even that to be found at Weston-Super-Mare's infamous beach. Meanwhile, a collection of scum-rings serve as grim Plimsoll lines to the bi-monthly activities of previous bloated bathers.

SHOUT

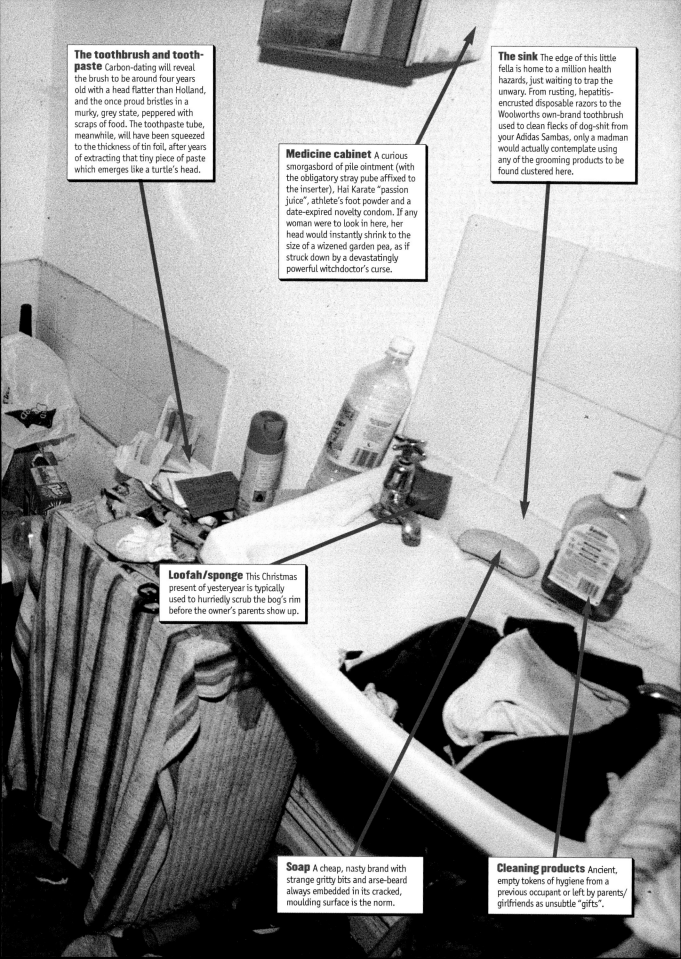

The toothbrush and toothpaste Carbon-dating will reveal the brush to be around four years old with a head flatter than Holland, and the once proud bristles in a murky, grey state, peppered with scraps of food. The toothpaste tube, meanwhile, will have been squeezed to the thickness of tin foil, after years of extracting that tiny piece of paste which emerges like a turtle's head.

Medicine cabinet A curious smorgasbord of pile ointment (with the obligatory stray pube affixed to the inserter), Hai Karate "passion juice", athlete's foot powder and a date-expired novelty condom. If any woman were to look in here, her head would instantly shrink to the size of a wizened garden pea, as if struck down by a devastatingly powerful witchdoctor's curse.

The sink The edge of this little fella is home to a million health hazards, just waiting to trap the unwary. From rusting, hepatitis-encrusted disposable razors to the Woolworths own-brand toothbrush used to clean flecks of dog-shit from your Adidas Sambas, only a madman would actually contemplate using any of the grooming products to be found clustered here.

Loofah/sponge This Christmas present of yesteryear is typically used to hurriedly scrub the bog's rim before the owner's parents show up.

Soap A cheap, nasty brand with strange gritty bits and arse-beard always embedded in its cracked, moulding surface is the norm.

Cleaning products Ancient, empty tokens of hygiene from a previous occupant or left by parents/ girlfriends as unsubtle "gifts".

The bog brush Having never seen any active service other than as a piss deflector, the bog brush's original colour is impossible to detect beneath its thick crust of dried, resinous urine. Likewise, the shitty water to be found inside contains so much "silt" that it has successfully fossilised the many unfortunate flies who choose it as their final, grim resting place.

Toilet paper One thing on Mother Earth is as constant as gravity itself: the scary bathroom never, ever has any serviceable bog roll – although there are always more than enough discarded cardboard innards to craft a lifesize space shuttle. In the absence of *bona fide* butt-wipe is an array of napkins, newspaper and grotesque magnolia flannels. Of course, guests only ever notice this fact too late.

The khazi More skidded than the mouth to any Paris underpass, the porcelain chute is quite literally a living mural to a thousand late-night takeaways – from both ends of its sorry owner. The only attempt made to remove these "Barry Sheenes" is when their blurry-eyed owner amuses himself by trying to forcefully piss them off with his first-thing-in-the-morning, battery acid urine.

U CAN'T FLUSH THIS!

Tired of boring enamel? Try easy-wipe gold fittings instead...

Of all the obscene bathrooms in the world, the one belonging to failed, baggy-trousered rapper MC Hammer must arguably be the worst, proving that not even he was too legit to shit. After raking in over $20 million from the sales of *Please Hammer Don't Hurt 'Em*, he blew his stack on a Boeing 727, a collection of 17 cars and, for some reason, nine fridges. But the highlight of Hammer's 12-acre mansion outside San Francisco was undoubtedly the absurd bathroom, which was the size of a sub-continent and was rumoured to have cost around £500,000. Inside was a jacuzzi as big as Lake Windermere, a sink like a bath and solid gold fittings throughout, right down to the 24-carat toilet seat.

EVERY MOTHER'S NIGHTMARE!

They've fed you, clothed you, pampered you for years, but you can't even remember your parents' birthdays. Exactly how crap a son *are* you?

YOU VIEW YOUR parents the way cats view their owners – an endless source of food and comfort, with no need to offer anything in return but your occasional presence. Since babyhood, you've sponged off your mum and dad, expected them to take time off work when you were ill, drive 300 miles to bail you out when you got arrested and simply support everything you do – however feeble-minded and dim your behaviour.

Yet despite demanding their unconditional love and ongoing fascination with you, you've barely spared a thought for their needs since you last made the old girl a potato-print card. You know nothing about the past, hopes and fears of the strangers who reared you, other than those that directly affect you. You've forgotten that they too are human beings, with passions and worries of their own. You should be ashamed that you know so little about them. You should, if you're a good son, be able to answer at least 20 of our questions. If you can't, wise up slacker!

THE PARENTS QUIZ

1. When and where did your parents first meet?
2. Name the boyfriend your mum had before meeting your dad.
3. What exams did your mum take at school or college?
4. What were your parents' first jobs?
5. What were their greatest ambitions when they were your age?
6. When is their wedding anniversary?
7. What was/is "their song"?
8. What religion did your dad grow up with?
9. Where were each of them born?
10. Name your dad's best friend at school or college.
11. What serious illnesses (including measles, mumps, etc) has your mum suffered from?
12. Does your dad have a talent he seldom uses? (Singing, stand-up comedy, writing, etc.)
13. What is your mum's favourite book?
14. Where was their first holiday together?
15. Does your mum have an irrational phobia?
16. What most depresses your dad?
17. What star sign are they both – and are they considered compatible astrologically?
18. What was their biggest row about?
19. What contraception do/did they use?
20. What do they both weigh?
21. Do either of them speak another language fluently?
22. Where did they always want to live, ideally?
23. Did your mum want kids before she had you?
24. What was the first record each of them bought?
25. Has either of them ever had an affair?

"Can I have some money, mumsy?"

REX

IN THE NAME OF LOVE

Like painters and musicians, the greatest sexual performers suffer for their art. So here's *FHM*'s guide to the ten biggest sexual adventurers of our time – plus, of course, the details of what happened to them…

10 The thrill of water swishing through his trunks got the better of Brazilian Claudiomiro Marques. While enjoying a swim at his local baths, Claudiomiro's eye was caught by a conveniently-sized filter to the side of the pool. He surreptitiously inserted his penis into the filter and prepared to enjoy the suction. Sadly, the pump was a little stronger than he'd anticipated and he was unable to withdraw. Doctors finally freed him, but not before knocking down part of the pool wall and taking some embarrassing snapshots.

Swimming pool filters: very public

9 Earl Zea, 34, said he was so frustrated at being stalked by a gay admirer that he sliced off his own penis with hedge-clippers. Both Zea and the man who was alleged to have stalked him later appeared on *The Jerry Springer Show*, with the "stalker" claiming the pair had once been lovers. Defending his actions, Zea explained that self-mutilation seemed the most effective way to make himself seem less attractive.

8 Frank Müller and his lover, Ulrike Stemmle, were both killed when the car they were having sex in plunged off a cliff. But the rapid descent to death was no

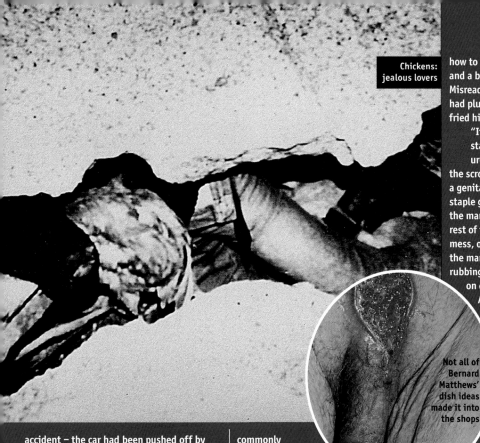

Chickens: jealous lovers

Not all of Bernard Matthews' dish ideas made it into the shops

how to make a sex toy from a cow's heart and a battery-powered electrical circuit. Misreading the instructions, the teenager had plugged directly into the mains – and fried himself to death.

"It was twice the size of a melon and it stank." That was how Pennsylvanian urologist William A Morton described the scrotum of a man who had tried to treat a genital wound by stapling his sac with a staple gun. On examination, doctors found the man's left testicle was missing and the rest of the genital area a lacerated, mangled mess, oozing pus and blood. After surgery, the man admitted he had injured himself by rubbing his penis against a canvas drive-belt on one of the machines in his workshop. As he reached orgasm, he caught his scrotum between the pulley wheel and the belt and had a testicle tossed several feet across the floor. Too embarrassed to admit how the accident had occurred, he stapled up the wound and continued working.

Contentedly enjoying carnal relations with a chicken in some hills near his home in Orense, Spain, a 39-year-old man was unaware that the huge rock situated above him was loose. The vibrations caused by the man's vigorous thrusting into the fowl caused the boulder to unbalance and land on top of the multi-species couple. Both perished.

accident – the car had been pushed off by Stemmle's husband Klaus, who had spotted it rocking back and forth near their home in Mönchengladbach. "I peered through the window and saw Ulrike with her dress down," explained Klaus, who had thought of Müller as his best friend before discovering the infidelity. The car exploded when it hit the bottom of the 150ft cliff.

Kim Lee Chong is currently serving a 15-year sentence in a Thai jail for having sex with a five-tonne elephant called Boua. Chong, 61, told the court that he recognised the elephant as the reincarnation of his wife, who had died 30 years earlier. Determined to remake his acquaintance with his missus, he clambered onto a wooden box and mounted the pachyderm from behind.

Ignoring all warnings not to try at home what you see on the screen, a man from Thurston County, Washington ended up with a broken swizzle-stick wedged in his member. The man, an avid consumer of porn movies, had earlier watched a film in which an actor had stimulated himself by ramming a cotton bud up his Jap's eye. Determined to recreate the scene, the man went home and, unable to find any cotton buds, employed the glass swizzle-stick instead, which duly shattered and sliced through his shaft. He was still in agony when the local fire brigade arrived an hour later.

A 45-year-old London man deliberately applied electrodes to his old fella. Emulating a torture technique more commonly employed by secret police forces around the world, the man had inserted two wires into a wall-socket then fixed them to his genitals. At least he survived, which is more than most torture victims can boast.

Man's best friend proved to be the undoing of Christopher Coulter during a sex session with his wife Emily. After smearing his genitals with peanut butter, Mr Coulter suggested that the couple invite in the family's Irish setter to lick it off. Unfortunately, the dog started ripping his master's cock to pieces, only ceasing its feeding frenzy when Mrs Coulter threw a bottle of perfume at the peanut butter-crazed hound, by which time the penis was completely severed. The member was eventually retrieved from the dog's jaws and reattached to Mr Coulter in hospital.

Called to a fire in Knoxville, Tennessee, emergency services discovered the naked corpse of a 16-year-old boy. They also found a cow's heart wired to the lad's testicles. The mystery was resolved when a search of the room uncovered a copy of *Ovid Now* magazine, which gave instructions on

Elephants: strangely familar

French bulldog An unsightly, flat-faced breed, which like the French themselves requires minimum grooming, is staggeringly ugly, and is of little or no value to the human race. Prone to the occasional bout of histrionics, too. *What it says about you One of the few blots on God's animal catalogue, ownership of the French bulldog indicates an appreciation of the hideous and, perhaps more disturbingly, a love of all things Gallic.*

Bull mastif

...ng between ... muscular mutt was bred ... gamekeepers to ward off poachers, pinning them down using only its legs. *What it says about you A man of few words, you ... ss do all the talking and ... nd with heavy-handed vi ... you really have to. You'll take ... all-comers, safe in the knowle ... that you'll always come out ... Own a bull mastif and people will respect you for the brooding beefcake you undoubtedly are.*

R. SMITH / NATURAL SCIENCE PHOTOS

Bedlington terrier Numb-skulled, lamb-like beast unlike any other terrier. Flighty and foolhardy, it's the Paul Gascoigne of the canine world — only quicker over ten yards and with a more tolerant attitude to the opposite sex. **What it says about you** *If the girl of your dreams sees you with this laughable excuse for an animal, you can safely assume she'll find you about as desirable as a warm can of Kestrel for breakfast.*

ONE MAN

Shih-tzu Faintly-rude sounding Oriental mutt that's believed to be descended from the lion that Buddha himself kept chained up in his backyard. Utter rubbish, clearly. **What it says about you** *The Shih-tzu needs precious little exercise, making it ideal for the slob. And the Buddhist connection may lend the sad an "exotic" reputation.*

The Labrador retriever Perennial favourite of children's TV shows, bog-roll advertisers and the blind, the Labrador retriever continues to be one of the most popular dogs in Britain. **What it says about you** *You're dependable, eager to please and very easy to manipulate. In short, you're one of life's losers — people are poking fun at you even as you're reading this.*

Rottweiler

Caesar's legions were fond of the rott, as while the dogs ran about the provinces biting chunks out of petrified villagers, the Romans got to put their sandalled feet up and eat grapes. Experts will tell you the dog is not naturally vicious – which, frankly, is bollocks.

What it says about you
You're insecure, have difficulty forging relationships with other human beings and possess a penis the size of a kidney bean.

Pug

Pug This uncaring, unthinking slut of a dog was originally bred by Buddhist monks and, like them, it's thoroughly miserable. The pug arrived in Europe in the 16th century, when the little bastard stowed away on ships of the Dutch East India Company.
What it says about you *Keeping one of these stocky dumptrucks indicates that you have as much difficulty making friends as Genghis Khan did.*

AND HIS DOG

The awful truth about the old adage is that for many men their dog really is their best friend. So what does your mutt say about you?

Great Dane Not Danish at all, but rather the chosen pet of Teutonic nobility. Often called the German dog, it's a towering beast of an animal capable of swallowing under-fives in one gulp. Often mistaken for a horse.
What it says about you *You're a man who respects his animal, who knows his own mind and will only ever resort to violence when there is no other avenue to pursue. You appreciate power, control and your car – and it's more than likely the class and comfort of the Ford Mondeo reflects that fact.*

Toy poodle

The kind of mutt you could easily crush to death if walking around your house in the small hours with the lights off. And in all honesty, you'd *want* to crush it to death. With its pathetic pointy face, fragile frame and hairdo more ludicrous than Pat Butcher's, it's no more a dog than your duvet.

What it says about you
You're dangerously effeminate, incredibly vain and can't be bothered to walk a dog. Which – given that the poodle isn't worth walking – is a stroke of luck.

Bouvier des Flandres

This noncey pooch, placid and unruffled, is arguably one of the most boring dogs on the planet, having little interest in retrieving sticks and/or chasing cats.
What it says about you *You're a man at home with being at home, who likes nothing better than sitting in an easy chair.*

"You can have it tomorrow"

"Never a borrower or a lender be," said the bard in one of his works. That might have been possible in the easy-going 1600s, but here in the 20th century we all live on credit. If you're flush, you lend your mates a few bob. If, however, they are a bit lazy in payback, you might want to follow our handy guidelines to getting your cash back.

■ **Stay calm** Those who owe you are likely to be defensive, offensive or both. You are probably not the only person that they owe, so make sure you're at the head of the queue and that you ask them, reasonably, to pay you back.

■ **Listen to the debtor** You are likely to have to negotiate.

Listen and suggest instalments. Ensure that any agreement is in writing. If you don't listen to the debtor, you could end up getting nothing back at all.

■ **Make sure the debtor knows you mean business** Ensure they remember they owe you. You can do this by dropping constant reminders and letting everybody else know that they owe you money. Embarrassment is always a great motivator.

■ **Check your legal standing** Get hold of some legal mumbo jumbo to support your threats of what will happen to him if he fails to pay up. This is likely to scare him and ensure he stops playing games. Hardly

anyone knows the law.

■ **Make sure that you use legal methods of collection** Avoid harassment and baseball bats: you'll certainly end up in court and possibly in jail. Getting yourself into grief over someone else's debt is just plain stupid.

■ **Use agencies** If you haven't the time to chase debts, there

are agencies who will write letters and make calls for you. This may cost you a percentage of your recovered debt, but cuts out a lot of the grief.

■ **Go to court and sue the debtor** This does, however, cost, and doesn't guarantee you'll see any cash – ensure the debtor has the funds to pay.

Ken's comedy crucifixion never failed to amuse the Christians

---

"Is that the time?"

Why be the free-spending life and soul of the party when you can just as easily sponge off everyone else?

The Tailender

Technique Cold-hearted and analytical method favoured by stats boffins and based loosely on the laws of probability. Simply ensure that you're the last one in the group to put your hand in your pocket to buy a round. For instance, if you are out with four friends, then by all means buy the fifth round – because the likelihood is that by the time you get round to the tenth pint, your colleagues will be: a) too pissed to remember whose round it is; b) slumped in a gutter; c) home in bed.

Strengths Your reputation as a convivial, generous fellow will be preserved, because you will at least be seen buying a round.

Weaknesses The main flaw of

the Tailender is the fact that you will have to buy a drink at all. **Rating: 7/10.**

The Bladder Bluff

Technique Head for the boozer at breakneck pace and charge inside, all the time moaning that you're bursting for a piss and adding "Mine's a pint of Stella!" as you disappear into the gents.

Strengths Even if you return to the bar and nobody has seen fit to get you a pint, you've only got to shell out for your own bevy.

Weaknesses Try this too often and you'll become a laughing stock among your chums for being a weak-bladdered, lily-livered gaylord who spends a curious amount of time in public toilets. **Rating: 6/10.**

The Doorman

Technique As you and your mates amble

towards the pub, forge ahead and open the door for the rest of your party. You'll be the last to the bar every time.

Strengths The Doorman is the cad's approach to round avoidance, displaying both impeccable manners and genius-like craftiness.

Weaknesses If it's raining, you'll be the one getting wet as your mates pile in; and if your manners at other times don't measure up, the ploy may swiftly be rumbled. **Rating: 8/10.**

The Lawrence Dodge

Technique Named after the legendary Victorian booze-shirker, Captain James "Dodger" Lawrence, who took to staring at the carpet in the billiards room at Singapore's famous Raffles Hotel whenever it was his turn to furnish his fellow officers with the pink gins. Simply stand at the bar staring intently at the floor, avoiding all eye and verbal contact. You can rest assured that someone will capitulate and get the beers in.

Strengths Reticence is the key, and the sound of your silence should be deafening.

Weaknesses The difficulty lies in trying to achieve a near-hypnotic state of almost Yogic trance, where only the phrase "What are you drinkin'?" will snap you out of it. **Rating: 6/10.**

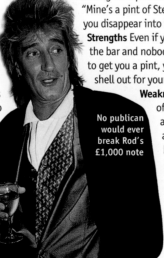

No publican would ever break Rod's £1,000 note

LIFE IMPROVING TIPS

THE A-Z OF PERVERSION

Vices for every letter of the alphabet. For no real reason

Axillism Armpit sex. For when orifices lose their sparkle.

Birds Avisodomists shag anything winged, then break their necks on attaining orgasm. Charming.

Capnolagnia Simply place the discarded butt of your loved one's cigarette in your mouth, and tug away.

Dancing Bell-dancing involves hanging fruit from hooks in one's skin, and dancing violently. Ideally, something heavier than grapes, but lighter than watermelons.

Excrement Coprophilia is the proper name for shit-smearing, eating or watching others dump from under a glass coffee table.

Felching Either sucking semen from an orifice, or inserting a de-clawed rodent up the arse (inside a condom). Remember to remove the guinea before that vital Monday morning presentation.

Giving sermons (homilophilia) A good fire and brimstone rant can bring on orgasm for the truly repressed. Possibly explains why Billy Graham remains popular.

Holes (aka furtling) Cut a hole in a picture of someone you fancy, stick your old man through, and voila!

Insects For a longer, more satisfying orgasm, get bees to sting the head of the penis – after ensuring you're not going to

Gloria wasn't asked back to the maypole

suffer from anaphylactic shock, of course.

Jacksy Utilised by the auto-pederast – a man with the ability to insert his penis into his anus. And get it out again, ideally.

Kennels One for the furries – people who pretend to be dogs... mating, rather than *Lady And The Tramp* spaghetti-sucking, usually.

Legs Some people have a sexual urge to have a limb amputated – apotemnophiles – while those who want sex with amputees are acrotomophiles. Not to mention, odd.

Meatotomy The widening of the urethra by cutting it over a long period, so that another man can stick his own (unmutilated) dick inside it. Meatotomists drew the short straw in the sexual lottery.

Nasophilia Arousal from anything to do with noses, from up the arse to sneezing on a willing partner.

Ochlophilia Pleasure gained from being in a crowd, pressing against strangers. Unless you're watching Millwall, of course.

Power tools The heady pleasure of drills, lathes and sanders. Quite a thrill, it's said – before you exsanguinate.

Quantity You need plenty of liquid for

"I'll fix your supper in a minute, Derek"

scrotal infusion. Fluid is pumped into the scrotum, where it leaks into the penis and balloons it to terrifying proportions. Result!

Roman showers Vomiting over a partner. Try wine, or lager and peanuts. Either way, no turn-on.

Snakes Used, generally by women, as sex toys. Small ones are best.

Trains (siderodromophilia) Ideally, sex in a moving carriage, rather than across a Hornby miniature track layout.

Used sanitary towels Said to turn some people on. Possibly ones who sleep in coffins and flinch at sunlight.

Vehicles There's a case of a man masturbating by the exhaust pipe of his Metro. Out of choice.

Women-crashing A Cambridge man cut brake cables – he would fantasise over women drivers losing control. Sane.

Xeroxing Flashing for the technically-minded.

Y The shape of lizard worshipped by some aborigines, who would split their penises in two. Without anaesthetic.

Zoophilia Sex with animals. Dogs and pigs are up for it. Apparently.

REX

EVERYBODY NEEDS GOOD NEIGHBOURS

The inhabitants of Ramsay Street obviously failed to take into account that council referral with a son who plays drums in a thrash metal band…

MANY PEOPLE, WHEN confronted with annoying neighbours, decide on swift and meticulous revenge. But simply tossing several pints of battery acid over their car isn't clever – and is highly illegal. Here are some more satisfying methods of revenge…

CUM ON FEEL THE NOIZE!
Noise complaints account for 70% of all neighbourhood disputes – yet Environmental Health officers are largely powerless to deal with troublesome neighbours with stereos like a Motörhead rig. However, the odds of getting a conviction can be stacked in your favour. If they're having a party, call the Environmental Health boys, saying you've complained yourself but were threatened. Next, call the noisy bastards and say that a bunch of irate neighbours, posing as local officials, are coming round to seize the stereo. The real jobsworths will be greeted with a fist, the police will be called and charges will be pressed. Result.
Likelihood of you getting trouble from the law *2/5. Depends whether the target can recognise your voice, so be careful.*
Effectiveness *2/5. Only real scum will attack the Bizzies.*

CHAIN LETTERS
The chain letter is nearly always a money-making scam. The letter should ask its recipients to send a pound to everyone on the list at the bottom of the page. Photocopy it 50 times and post around your neighbourhood. All of the names and addresses will be false – except one. And guess who that belongs to? A visit from the Bill is certain.
Likelihood of you getting trouble from the law *0/5. Just be careful not to leave any prints and ensure that it's totally anonymous.*

But be warned: sending chain letters is illegal.
Effectiveness *2/5. Your neighbour may be able to convince Plod of his innocence.*

TAMPER WITH THE ELECTRIC METER
This is easy if you have a shared hallway – the meters will usually be in a communal box. Simply cut a neighbour's meter security wire (the one with a lead slug crimped round one end to prevent tampering). Alternatively, perform the old council estate trick of placing a magnet over the meter's rotating flywheel, slowing it down and saving cash. Then, tip off the Electricity Board, saying you discovered your neighbour's "scam" while reading your own meter. But beware – they'll immediately suspect your neighbour's isn't the only one tampered with.
Likelihood of you getting trouble from the law *3/5. Illegal, and if the victim convinces the authorities it wasn't him, the suspicion will fall on other people in your unit.*
Effectiveness *2/5. The unneighbourly victim will only get a stiff talking to.*

SEND HIM SOME "FREE SAMPLES"
Those annoying free samples of toothpaste and the like delivered to your home can be doctored to suit the purposes of revenge. Replace toothpaste with Ralgex, washing powder with itching powder and aftershave with urine. Likewise, foul-smelling sprays can easily be disguised as air fresheners. Then pop them through your neighbour's door. They're sure to use them.
Likelihood of you getting trouble from the law *1/5. Wear gloves while handling the goodies and the only risk you run is if you're seen delivering the tainted goods.*
Effectiveness *1/5. Target may prefer their usual brand; users will be angry, not damaged.*

TRICK OR TREAT!
Get some local kids to visit his house, then stop them on the stairs. Acting horrified,

seize the fruit they've been given, cunningly sliding a razor blade into an apple. Alert police. Kiddie crime is so sensitive that irate locals may react violently toward a man who tried to kill toddlers with fruit. They may even run your unwanted neighbour out of town.
Likelihood of you getting trouble from the law *4/5. Your role is dangerously high-profile, and kids have a habit of singing like canaries.*
Effectiveness *4/5. Sweet little kids always stir up the emotions.*

FLOODING
Perfect if you live above the culprits and rent your flat. Leaving a bath running could leave you liable, so instead cunningly unscrew a pipe-fitting join and go out for the day. His carpets, floors, wallpaper and, hopefully, worldly possessions will be ruined.
Likelihood of you getting trouble from the law *5/5. If you crack under questioning you'll end up before the beak.*
Effectiveness *0/5 to 3/5 depending on where you live. You'll also damage your own pad.*

TIP OFF CUSTOMS
If your neighbour is planning a foreign jaunt, you can increase his chances of unpleasant attention from foreign Customs officials. Planting porn or drugs in his bags is risky and illegal, but a call to the Customs Office at his destination will do. Whisper something about "drugs… real hardcore… Mr Big". Local officials, used to calls from lowly grasses, will pull your hapless neighbour on touchdown, having first prepared fresh surgeons' gloves. Muslim countries may keep him for the duration of his stay.
Likelihood of you getting trouble from the law *0/5. As long as you dial 141 first.*
Effectiveness *4/5 if in the US; less elsewhere. The Italians will probably throw him a party.*

KOBAL

"Is that *your* fridge on the front lawn?"

READ YOUR GIRL

She may well be the most gorgeous woman you've laid your drunken eyes on,
Day, but the real test of her sexual compatibility will arrive when she reveals

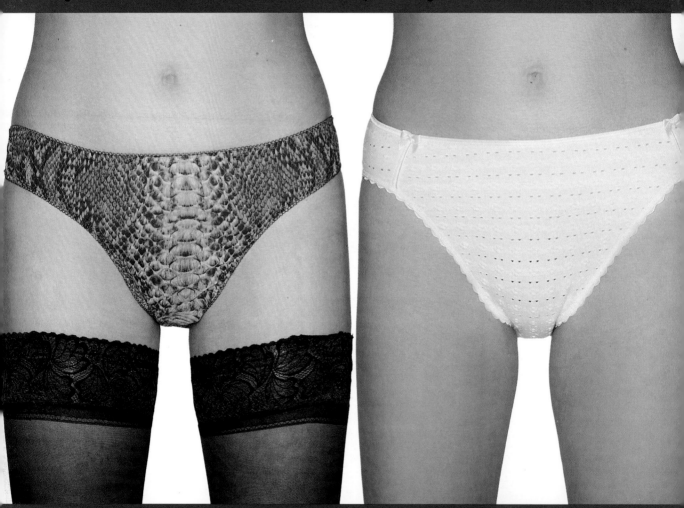

THE AGENT PROVOCATEUR PANT

Agent Provocateur make knickers for the woman who takes lingerie
seriously, the woman who's in total control of her own life, knows
what she wants in bed – and has got herself a boyfriend with more
money than sense. Ideal for keeping as a mistress, the Agent
Provocateur wearer knows and relishes her place in the sexual
scheme of things, and revels in the sensation of silk and satin
brushing between her milky thighs.

What to do if encountered *You've got to recognise that this woman
is a sexual predator, someone who enjoys the high life, and that if
you can't keep up with her demands – both physical and fiscal – then
your services will be dispensed with. Sharpish.*

THE SENSIBLE PANT

Everyday underwear for the practical girl, the major flaw of the
sensible small is the tendency to grip less-toned cheeks, creating the
dread "visible panty line". That said, these are the briefs of the girl
your mother would dearly love you to settle down with, and if you're
at that stage of your life when you can no longer be bothered with the
thrill of the chase, then fine – dive in. If you're not, dive in anyway,
because as long as you can cope with her broken heart and
innumerable tearful pleas for reconciliation, you should be okay.

What to do if encountered *Think long and hard about what you
really want from life. These may only be a pair of pants, but they could
spell the end of your days on the singles circuit.*

FRIEND'S PANTS

while she thinks you're the most magnificent physical specimen since Darren
her pants for the very first time. Here's what you're letting yourself in for...

THE ANN SUMMERS PANT

A short step away from peephole bras and crotchless knickers, these supposedly sexy smalls are generally favoured by swingers in Basingstoke and by women whose housekeeping money won't stretch to La Perla. If you've noticed that your girlfriend wears this kind of impractical gear on a daily basis, then it's more than likely she's either having an affair with a colleague, or contemplating a career in the specialist magazine industry.

What to do if encountered *Be very, very wary. Go home with this woman and you'll probably be greeted at the front door of her new-build home by her husband, Terry, wearing nothing but a leopard-print thong and a broad grin.*

THE BELLY-WARMER

These unflattering, nappy-like pants are favoured by grannies, members of the Christian Outreach Church and turnip-breathed women from the former Eastern Bloc. At a stretch, the belly-warmer can be pulled way beyond the hips to provide extra insulation for the breasts, nipples and upper torso. They're also effective for holding a girl's gut in. Be warned, though: date a woman who wears these and you'll have sex no more than once a week and only receive oral gratification on your birthday.

What to do if encountered *Ask her to cease undressing immediately and put her kit back on. Then take her by the hand, lead her to the front door and point her in the direction of the nearest taxi rank.*

HOW TO THROW AN ORGY
Be a swinger

Ulrika would do anything for Swedish/Japanese relations

■ **Who to invite?** Any beautiful and open-minded couples – particularly single women you know. People to avoid are any handsome, unattached men, and the bloke from the footie team who's hung like a baboon.

■ **Decor** First, scrupulously tidy your flat, because nobody will thank you for "crumb rash" on their exposed derrière. Tack up some tasteful nudes, change the sheets and light some scented candles to mask any unpleasant pongs. Subdued lighting increases confidence, but overdo it and you could partake in an unexpected game of blind man's buff – remember, there are "man holes" lurking.

■ **Food and drink** Take a tip from the Romans, who used to prepare sexually provocative snacks, such as breast-shaped blancmanges and phallic pastries called *colyphia*. Classic aphrodisiacs, such as oysters and caviar, are dynamite, if costly. As for grog, your best bet is loads of red wine or a rum punch loaded with fruit juice to mask its killer strength. Avoid refried bean burritos, real ale and anything containing brussels sprouts.

■ **Games** Warm-up games are essential to help break the ice: passing an apple around using only the mouth or getting a girl to inflate a balloon placed inside a man's pants, for instance.

■ **Music** The tunes, like the booze, should keep on flowing. But beware: while Seventies-style porn music compilations add authenticity, dance mixes can get plain tiring. Classical music, such as Ravel's *Bolero* – as used by Bo Derek in *10* – also goes down well. And for God's sake, plan ahead: if the tape auto-flicks onto your dad's *British Song Birds Collection* in the other deck, dicks will wilt quicker than a Glaswegian in Greece.

■ **Accessories** A softish porn movie and bowls of condoms are probably all that's required. Dildos the size of elephants' legs, hardcore, shit-eating, German porno flicks and interconnected gasmasks should be avoided at all costs. Unless you know for sure your guests will like them.

HOW TO STAND FOR PARLIAMENT
"I'm committed to the welfare state"

Have you ever sat at home and wondered just who on Earth the people who run this country think they are? Do they know what they are doing? They do, it's true, appear to be quite insane most of the time, so why not do something about it? You could, in theory, be sitting down next to Harriet Harmen and David Blunket and debating whether or not we should be allowed to drink water and eat cheese. All you have to do is follow our guide to attaining power...

White suits: daft

■ **Make sure you're eligible** Certain people aren't allowed to stand for Parliament. If you are a convicted criminal who has served more than a year, a member of the clergy, a baron, a duke, someone who is deaf and dumb, someone who is mentally ill, or not British, you can't stand.

■ **Look presentable** Experts reckon that Richard Nixon lost the 1960 US Presidential election because his top lip was sweaty during an interview with eventual winner John F. Kennedy. If you want the people to take you seriously, get yourself a makeover.

■ **Formalities** You need nomination papers with ten signatures and £50 from each person who has signed it. Take this to the town hall that's organising the constituency vote.

LIFE IMPROVING TIPS

■ **Pick your constituency** To win a seat you need at least 15% of the votes. To have a chance of getting those votes, aim for a seat somewhere with a small number of voters and make sure you're a memorable candidate.

■ **Avoid scandal** If you do have skeletons in your cupboard, either reveal them before you start your campaign in an act of selfless honesty, or make sure there isn't a chance in Hell that the tabloids can get hold of them. Being out in front in the polls, only to lose because your affair with an 80-year-old millionairess is revealed, is a gutter.

■ **Be realistic** You might really want to redirect all of the arms budget to the homeless, but at most points in a nation's history you're going to find this a very unpopular campaign promise. Be moderate, and focus on the key issues: education, the health service and law and order.

3 MINUTES TO PARTY!

Should Armageddon come knocking at your door, how best to fill those last 180 seconds? Get these in for when the sirens wail…

LITERATURE

Any book will have to approached from either the front or the back – any time wasted flicking through for the "good bits" will doubtless result in disappointment. Also, avoid reference books, as Forfar's average home game attendance and Middlesbrough's goal difference is neither useful nor entertaining when The Reaper comes a-knocking. Try a cult classic like *The Dice Man* or *American Pyscho* – two books that laugh at death.

Books: better not start a new one

DRINK

Forget about putting the kettle on – a full bottle of tequila or vodka should be grabbed and guzzled straight from the neck. If it starts to hurt, then try a chaser in the form of one of those super-strength lagers favoured by tramps. Avoid "nicely kept" woodcasked bitters and those tiny bottles of French lagers girls buy for barbecues.

Lager: straight from the can

FOOD

The only diet you'll need is The Death Plan: cake and steak. Mind you, there's not much time to cook your meat, so bung it in the oven on top heat for two minutes and stick your face in a Black Forest gateau while you wait. Don't bother phoning Dominos, either – there might be a rush on.

ART

If you're of an artistic bent, you may not want to indulge in total hedonism, so why not peruse a relevant painting while the sky reddens outside. . Holbein's The Ambassadors is particularly poignant, as a close second look reveals that the smudge at the bottom is really a bloody great skull thing; while a picture of dogs playing pool will have you howling with laughter.

VIDEOS

Fast-forwarding is going to take too much time, so pick a film that rocks from start to finish. *Apocalypse Now*, *Rambo* and the totally illegal *A Clockwork Orange* have great opening scenes, as do most porn flicks – a few minutes is all it takes before the pizza delivery boy drops his deep-pan Seafarer and gets down to business. For opening minutes of sport, Alan Shearer's goal against Germany in Euro 96 is hard to beat, as is the *Mike Tyson's Greatest Hits* video package. But Arsenal fans may think that fast-forwarding for two minutes is worth it for the chance of glimpsing Michael Thomas's championship winner at Anfield one last time.

PHONE CALLS

If you fancy a chat on the phone before the end, then forget it – none of your mates will be in a fit state to converse. A sex line, on the other hand, could be just what you need – and the extortionate cost and embarrassing itemised bill won't ever enter into the equation. Just make sure you don't dial one that takes three minutes before she's said anything filthier than her name.

SMOKES

This is one occasion that doesn't suit the ultra-low or peppermint lady-fag – what you want is a big ole Cuban cigar. And although there's enough tobacco in one of these gaspers to kill a horse, only a full hit will do on Judgement Day. Three minutes of this and your lungs will feel like blackened banana skins. But, hey – who cares?

Cigars: don't worry about an ashtray

SEX

The pre-Apocalypse shagger shouldn't care less if his woman is from next door, never mind Venus. No foreplay. No undressing. And if you suffer from premature ejaculation and want to take your mind off the task in hand, then simply visualise the state the both of you will be in once the blast wave's hit. Of course, it may take a while to persuade a panicking woman on the street to join you, so if you're on your tod, Madame Palm and her five sisters is the answer. Fast and furious – pull your old chap up and down like a bicycle pump.

NICOLE EX VEGAS STRIPPER

0171 – 913 6582

GENUINE PHOTO

2 MINS

Sex: forget the foreplay

MUSIC

Pop can provide the perfect soundtrack to imminent death, so if you're going to go, go with a bang. Three minutes isn't long – better avoid anything by prog-rockers or smart-alec Germans. Instead, try a punk rock classic: short, sweet and loud, you can welcome the Four Horsemen with two fingers. The Damned's *New Rose* or Motörhead's *Ace Of Spades* should do the job.

The Damned: your soundtrack to Apocalypse

THE FHM IQ TEST

You might not get a prize, like the cut-glass bowl William G. Stewart hands out after the final of *Fifteen To One*, but come out tops in The FHM IQ Test and you'll win something money can't buy: the knowledge that not only can you do maths and stuff, but that you also get out the house every now and then

FHM KNOWLEDGE

1 According to the FHM Sex Quiz for Men, what was the average length of a British man's penis?

1a And how many times a week does he have sex?

2 Who is the current FHM World's Sexiest Woman?

3 What about last year?

4 Who was the highest new entry in '98?

5 In February's FHM, what colour was Kylie Minogue's unforgettable see-through chiffon slip?

6 Which of the following beauties was not an FHM cover star in 1998?
a) Rhona Mitra
b) Melanie Sykes
c) Dannii Minogue

7 Which of these "comedians" was not lambasted in FHM's captions this year?
a) Lenny Henry
b) Ben Elton
c) Roy Walker

8 In Reporter, we feature many weird museums. Which of the following have museums in their honour?
a) Menstruation
b) Barbed wire
c) Dirt

9 Who is the only Reporter Babe in the history of FHM who once had a penis?

10 Which of the following sexual perversions has Grub Smith not

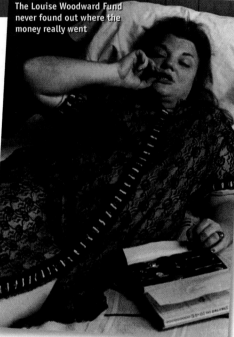

The Louise Woodward Fund never found out where the money really went

tried this year?
a) Being anally intruded by a woman wearing a strap-on dildo
b) A wine enema
c) Necrophilia

11 Which of the following activities was not included in June's sports that ought to die feature?
a) Bowls
b) Darts
c) UK American football

12 In one of FHM's most famous pictures, a dead man is having sexual intercourse with which farmyard animal?
a) A sheep
b) A pig
c) A chicken

13 How heavy was the ovarian cyst removed from the woman featured in FHM's gruesome illnesses feature?
a) 21 stone 7lb
b) 14 stone 8lb
c) 32 stone 3lb

14 According to FHM's March hair special, what should balding men never do?
a) Grow it long and tie it in a ponytail
b) Shave it all off
c) Tease a slow one out in public

15 The earthquake victim trapped in the mangled wreckage of her car in March's True Life screamed what to her rescuers?

16 In April's Weird Sex feature, what strange trick could Freddy the dolphin perform with his phallus?

17 And in the same feature, what unfortunate animal was dressed in sexy lingerie by a pervy zoo keeper?

18 After which film star did Britain's maddest convict name himself?
a) Kenneth Branagh
b) Clint Eastwood
c) Charles Bronson

19 Which of the following weren't among his hostage demands?

SEX AND RELATIONSHIPS

1 **You're taking a woman on a first date. Where do you go?**
a) A Slayer gig
b) A nice restaurant
c) You ask her for ideas

2 **The bill arrives. What do you do?**
a) Produce your portable abacus
b) Slap down your gold card, saying: "Everywhere accepts that colour!"
c) Offer to pay in full, but let her stump up her half if she insists

3 **Rubber johnnies...**
a) Are essential for penetrative sex in the caring Nineties
b) Are around here somewhere
c) Are too small for you

4 **A woman's clit responds best to:**
a) A good, frantic frigging
b) Small electrical charges
c) Gentle caressing with a darting tongue-tip

5 **A basque is...**
a) A machine gun-toting, bomb-throwing, maniacal Spaniard
b) A delicious lobster-based soup
c) A figure-enhancing corset for the female's upper torso

VERBAL LINGUISTICS

1 **Underline the two words that are the closest in meaning:**
Gascoigne, house, road, sky, buffoon

2 **Find the odd one out among the following selection:**
Leeds, Manchester, Liverpool, London, Sheffield

3 **Which beer is the odd one out?**
Kestrel, Kilkenny's, Kaliber, Kronenburg, Kirin

4 **Which popular snack product is the odd one out?**
Monster Munch, Quavers, Wotsits, Frisps, Skips

5 **Underline the word which makes the sentence most generally true:**
A woman is (clever, attractive, childbearing, female, annoying)

...rry would do ...ything to pick ... Jazz FM

a) An Uzi
b) A getaway car
c) An apple pie

20 **In April's meat vs veg feature, which of the following meat dishes wasn't considered a delicacy?**
a) Glazed dormouse
b) Seal-brain fritters and deep-fried flipper
c) Rabbit's eye soup

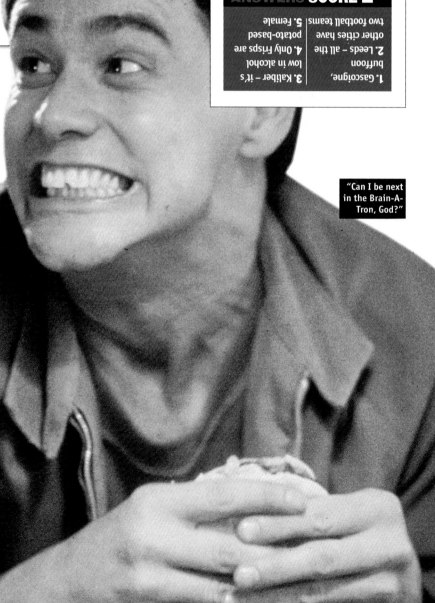

"Can I be next in the Brain-A-Tron, God?"

1 Mobile phones are:
a) Essential fashion items to be toyed with at every opportunity
b) For total twats
c) Useful in an emergency

2 Throwing a drink-related "food poisoning" sicky is:
a) Totally deplorable behaviour – a sackable offence
b) Acceptable every now and then – everyone else is at it
c) Essential on a Monday morn – I get paid peanuts anyway!

3 You work because...
a) Your career defines your very existence
b) It pays for the rent and booze
c) Dad's been giving you grief about the stack you owe him

4 You're going out to a club for the night. What do you wear?
a) A long-sleeved, hooded and baggy "Rave On" T-shirt/dungaree combo

Food poisoning: essential?

b) Flares, an afro wig, stick-on sideburns
c) The same Port Vale shirt you've been wearing all day

5 What is Freddie Starr?
a) A shining beacon of laughter; a maverick Great British comic
b) An unfunny, abattoir-creeping, pigeon-chested, bilious, child-beating Scouse twat
c) A hamster-eating, madcap, zany livewire

ANSWERS SCORE ■
1. c 2. b 3. b 4. None of these – they're all equally offensive 5. b

1 Complete the following line from a well-known yogurt ad jingle: "This is the captain of your ship...
a) ...hyperventilating"
b) ...calling"
c) ...Brian"

2 Who did Nicole jolt at the altar in this year's Renault ad?
a) Bobby Davro
b) Hugh Grant
c) Vic Reeves

3 Which of these men have not been linked with Ulrika Jonsson?
a) Hunter
b) Stan Collymore
c) Chris Evans

4 Which of these TV personalities does not wear a hairpiece?
a) Paul Daniels
b) Terry Wogan
c) Brucie

5 What variety of kebab was Gazza caught eating just days before he was axed from the England squad?
a) Meat
b) Shish
c) Chicken

6 What time was Teddy Sheringham out until just days before the tournament kicked off?
a) 6.45am
b) 5.30am
c) 2.37am

7 Who of the following have not been found guilty of killing a child?
a) Myra Hindley
b) Louise Woodward
c) Peter Sutcliffe

8 Which of the following is a genuine malt whisky?
a) Glengregory
b) Glenmorangie
c) Glencampbell
d) Glenoddle
e) Glenmadeiros

9 Which of the following meats is it illegal to buy in Britain?
a) Crocodile
b) Kangaroo
c) Horse

10 What is the UK's most popular curry dish?
a) Chicken madras
b) Tandoori armadillo
c) Chicken tikka masala

11 What was the car called in the Dukes Of Hazzard?
a) General Lee
b) Colonel Bogie
c) Good 'Ol Boy

1 State whether the conclusions in the statements below are certainly true. If certainly not true, they're false
a) My father and brothers booze a lot, therefore I booze a lot
b) All pants are good. I have some pants, therefore they are good
c) Some Jocks are tight. Some old people are tight. Therefore, some Jocks are old people
d) There are more terms of abuse in Derby than in Leeds
e) Trevor has a big stick. Therefore Trevor is scary

2 Reg has three chicken tikka masalas, one of which he knows has E-coli in it. Which of the following can he say for certain?
a) "If I eat all these rubies, I will get ill"
b) "If I eat all the curries and die, I will know the bacteria were deadly"
c) "It's safer not to eat any of the curries"
d) "I can safely eat two of the curries"
e) "The waiter who served me these rubies was trying to kill me!"

3 Which two phrases are most similar in meaning?
a) "Right, this is absolutely my last drink, okay everyone?"
b) "I can't, I'm baby-sitting for my sister"
c) "Sorry! Badminton practice tonight"
d) "I'm bushed. It's an early night for me"
e) "Right, less of the chit-chat, let's get trousered!"

4 You suspect your girlfriend is having it away with Barry from the petrol station. She denies it. Who is best to ask whether she's lying her cheating socks off?
a) Someone who is occasionally truthful
b) Someone who is often truthful
c) Someone who's never truthful

5 Is the following conclusion true or false?
All Brummies are bores. All Scousers are thieves. Some thieves are Brummies. Some numbskulls are Scousers. Therefore some bores are thieves

6. Mr Lager has already appeared in this book. Where?

ANSWERS SCORE ■
1. FFFF 2. c 3. a and e 4. c) 5. T 6. p34

REX, KOBAL

12 Which football commentator retired after this year's World Cup?
a) Motto
b) Brian Moore
c) Barry Davies

13 In the film *Deliverance*, which actor suffers the misfortune of being anally violated while tied to a tree?

14 Which queen of country music died this year?

15 What are Embassy World Darts champ Ray Barneveld's nicknames?

16 The name of which Motörhead album was derived from a Woody Allen film?

17 What is the most widely recognised trademark in the world?

18 What was the score in England's record rugby union defeat by the mighty Wallabies last year?

19 What is the highest-grossing movie of all time?
a) *Titanic*
b) *Gone With The Wind*
c) *Swiss Family Robinson*

20 In what year did the 20p piece come into circulation?

21 During which show did Tommy Cooper pop his clogs?
a) *Hot Shoes* with Wayne Sleep
b) *Rock With Laughter* with Bobby Davro
c) *The Royal Variety Performance* with Eammon Andrews

22 Who are the three presenters of the awesome Blankety Blank?

23 Who are the stars of The Magnificent Seven?

24 Name the A&R man who turned down the Beatles

25 Which football team has outraged the nation by attempting to buy Wembley Stadium?

"Balti? Or pop it in in the tandoor?"

26 How long was John Holmes' dick?

27 Which is the fake beer?
a) Bishop's Finger
b) Vicar's Digit
c) Hairy Helmet

28 Which Jock scored an own goal for Brazil?

29 Which of the following cowards has beaten a woman?

Allen: metalhead

a) Tommy Lee
b) Stan Collymore
c) Paul Gascoigne

30 Which of the following is not a sex substitute for women?
a) Chocolate
b) Shopping
c) Backgammon

31 Which of the following is not a breakfast cereal?
a) Malted Monkeys
b) Count Chocula
c) King Vitamin

32 True or false: giraffes cannot lie down

33 Where would you find the mighty pike?
a) In a murky pond
b) In an open ocean
c) Gospel Oak Lido

34 True or false: a cheese cob idly tossed from the top of Blackpool Tower could kill a man

35 True or false: Chuck Berry installed hidden cameras in his night-club's latrines

36 Which is the real designer?
a) Tony Boss
b) Kendo Nagasaki
c) Tommy Nutter

37 Which of these is not commonly found inside a toilet cistern?
a) A ballcock
b) A float arm
c) A plastic bag full of £50 notes

38 Which of the following is a bona fide Jeffrey Archer novel?
a) *For A Few Dollars Maureen*
b) *Bigger Than The Bible*
c) *Not A Penny More, Not A Penny Less*

39 Bill Clinton suffers from which rare disorder of the genitalia?
a) Peyronie's disease
b) Phallic syndrome
c) Rummenigge's Trichosa

40 Which of these is the real gangster?
a) Frankie "The Axe" Foreman
b) Toni "Knuckles" Dorrito
c) Boris "The Bastard" Shakeyernoboff

41 Which of the following foreign customs is bogus?
a) Eat and wipe your arse with different hands
b) Wedding-night sex as a family spectator sport
c) Late return of library books means a whipping

42 Which is not CB jargon?
a) "Bear in the air!"
b) "Smokey's ticklin' m' whiskers!"
c) "Hammer down!"

43 Which of these are not genuine burial gifts?
a) A packet of Marlboro
b) A cat
c) A star-spangled waistcoat and cravat combo

HOLY BIBLE

"It's brilliant, Jeffrey!"

44 Which of these is not a US wrestler?
a) Brutus "The Barber" Beefcake
b) Mike "The Maelstrom" Magnusson
c) "Hacksaw" Jim Duggan

45 Which of these is a real name for a magazine?
a) *Nails, Talons and Claws*
b) *Spincterian Quarterly*
c) *Laboratory Glassware News*

ANSWERS SCORE ■

	33. a	**16.** Orgasmatron	weaknesses,
32. False	Horst Buchholz,	Flying Postman	**7. c.** For all his
45. They are all real	**31.** a	McQueen,	Rubble or the	
	30. c	Bronson, Yul	**15.** Barney	**6.** a
44. b	**43.** c	Brynner, Steve	Wynette	**5. c**
42. b	shits	**23.** Charles	**14.** Tammy	syrup
41. c	**29.** All of the	Savage	**13.** Ned Beatty	longer wears his
40. a	**28.** Tommy Boyd	Les Dawson, Lily	**12.** b	Daniels no
39. a	**27.** b	**22.** Terry Wogan,	**11.** a	**4. a.** Paul
38. c	**26.** 14 inches	**21.** c	**10.** c	her
37. c	**25.** Arsenal	**20.** 1982	**9. c**	nights out with
36. c	**24.** Dick Rowe	**19.** a	**8.** b	all enjoyed
35. True	**18.** A 76-0	**17.** Coca-Cola	Sutcliffe stuck	**3. None: they've**
34. False	Eli Wallach	thrashing	to adults	**2. c**
	James Coburn,			**1.** b
	Robert Vaughn,			

Running Horses Inc

FHM BACHELOR GUIDE 117

NUMERICAL DEXTERITY

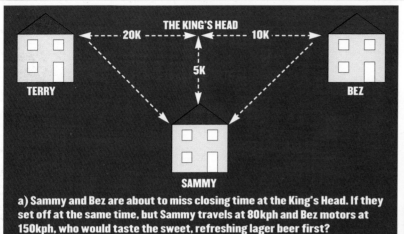

THE KING'S HEAD

20K — 10K

TERRY — 5K — BEZ

SAMMY

a) Sammy and Bez are about to miss closing time at the King's Head. If they set off at the same time, but Sammy travels at 80kph and Bez motors at 150kph, who would taste the sweet, refreshing lager beer first?
b) If it takes Terry half an hour to get to Bez's, what is his average speed?

2 If two bras and one strap-on jack costs ten quid, and two strap-ons and one bra costs eight quid, how much are:
a) Strap-on jacks
b) Bras

3 If you're left with £75 after giving four times the cost of the barrels in change to the bloke who bought five barrels of pale ale from you, how much did you charge per barrel?

4 You drunkenly arranged to meet a girl, but if Wednesday is the day after tomorrow, what day was the tomorrow of the day before yesterday when you set the date?

5 Nine is to 81 as seven is to... what?

Crowther chortled at his pale ale coup

CREATIVE ABILITY

1 Write down 20 words that rhyme with tank

2 Which snack is the odd one out?

Bag of chips, samosa, curry, burger

3 Using 12 matches, make the name of a well-known Australian pop star

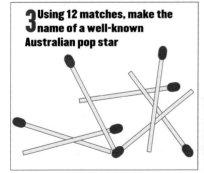

4 Which pint-pot is the odd one out?

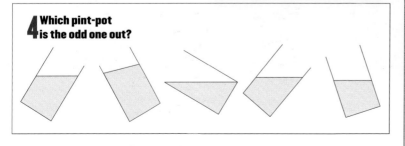

5 Draw the shortest route from The Nag's Head to The Taj Mahal

Nag's Head

Taj Mahal

MAN OR MORON?

76 AND OVER: Sing Hosannas! Sing! For truly you are a prince among men. You know a little bit about women, a smidgen about style and you've spent your time wisely absorbing the interesting morsels of life that make it worth living. You can probably take your ale, too. Either that, or you're an anally-retentive pub quiz bore who everybody loathes. Be warned.

45 TO 75: You're an average, ordinary Joe, the man on the street who enjoys everything in moderation and who should really get out a bit more. So, instead of sitting there of a Sunday afternoon with your trousers around your ankles, watching *The Clothes Show* in the vain hope of seeing a stray nipple, get out there and drink in everything life has to offer. You can and must do better.

45 AND UNDER: You bring shame and embarrassment to all whose lives you blight with your soulless banality. Including your family. Your idea of a stonking joke is when some student scrawls an "I" on a "TO LET" sign. You queue alone to buy the new Ben Elton best-seller. Wise up, sucker, or after a lifetime as a mouse you'll die, cold and alone, beneath a pile of old blankets.

REX

Sick of Madonnas and apple-cheeked Santas? Make your own card, then...

Jesus Loves Everybody

Even a miserable bastard like you

Ho bloody ho

Experience nirvana in your front room. Have sex! Watch TV!

The armchair has, for generations, been the site of many pleasurable masculine pursuits. Your grandfather sat, after a hard day's labour, studying the form at Chepstow in the *Sporting Life*. Your father spent many joy-filled hours watching *The Sweeney*, his face a picture of joy as he supped his Party Seven. Now it's your turn in the Big Chair – but what can it offer you? Not only is your lounge buddy the perfect platform from which to view cable TV and video games; the armchair can please your good lady, too. What's more, this 12-step plan for armchair action will in no way interfere with your televisual pleasure.

1. THE SIDEWINDER

Aim This position is the one you'll want if you are up for a long, hard session with the deepest penetration possible.
Method It's your basic doggy style, but knees are protected from carpet rash by the soft cushion of the chair. She uses the side of the chair for her arm supports, and you use her back. It's good if she keeps her bra on to gain some extra purchase for maximum thrust.
Difficulty 4/10
There is a small worry that she might suffer a slight abdominal strain, but this can be offset with a handy throw cushion. Absolutely perfect for those long, slow-moving programmes which require only an occasional glance – snooker, for instance.

2. THE PERSIAN KISS

Aim The Persian Kiss should give you maximum enjoyment from minimum effort.
Method You simply sit comfortably, feet firmly on the floor and legs akimbo, while your good lady kneels between your legs and engages you with her mouth.
Difficulty 1/10
This position is ideal for programmes which require your almost undivided attention: documentaries, perhaps, an arthouse movie, or anything hosted by Melvyn Bragg.

3. THE MIGHTY FLIPPER

Aim You want to be able to occasionally cast your eyes from the telly and admire your backside as it gets on with the job.
Method First of all, your girlfriend has to fall backwards from the chair, leaving her middle bit on the seat. You can enter her by keeping yourself off the floor with your arms.
Difficulty 7/10
There is a danger of see-sawing out of your woman if your arms buckle. This position is nice for a quickie during a cartoon: Ren And Stimpy should do it.

4. CUDDLE THE KOALA

Aim To achieve vaginal penetration, with the bonus of the occasional kiss and dirty whisper.
Method Your girlfriend will have to snuggle up to your seated form. With her arms wrapped around your back and head and body to one side, your viewing shouldn't be interrupted.
Difficulty 2/10 *You may find you are slightly distracted from the box by the almost instinctive bob and thrust of the pelvis. Good for quiz shows.*

5. RIP VAN WINKLE

Aim To be woken from a pleasant slumber just in time for a favourite show.
Method You lie crossways over your girlfriend's lap. She takes you in her mouth, waking you with a lovely, tingling oral alarm.
Difficulty 1/10
Your main concern here is that you are woken at precisely the right time. To this end, your girl should begin stimulation during the dull period prior to your show: Video Nation just before the darts would be perfect.

LAZY BOY LOVE

6. THE PINK FLAMINGO
Aim: Stay exactly in the Rip Van Winkle position. This one's a real challenge to your horny girlfriend.
Method Poised over your rampant stalk, your girl pivots with one foot braced steadily on the floor, the other raised over the arm of the chair, and impales herself for maximum intrusion.
Difficulty 5/10 *She'll have to have a ballerina's balance. Perhaps best suited for some videos on MTV. You can dip in and out of the visuals as you do your old lady.*

7. THE LAPPING HARE
Aim: Let's not forget the lady. A little lick can go a very long way. Plus, as a bonus, you get pulled off!
Method With both legs up over the back of the chair, your girlfriend's pudenda is near your flicking tongue. And look! Her hand is free for a pleasurable yank!
Difficulty 3/10 *Your lady's most private place could provide a welcome distraction from Noel Edmond's foul family frolics.*

8. FULL THROTTLE

Aim To express the physical excitement you get from the TV directly through your girlfriend's body.

Method Kneel on the arms of the chair as she braces against you by hooking her legs over the back. Now make like a bike.

Difficulty 8/10 *Balance and weight distribution are critical. This is great for a road movie: The Wild Ones would be spot-on.*

9. THE ROYAL COMMAND

Aim To stretch out your aching limbs at the end of the evening, with the novel dual benefit of schtupping the old lady.

Method Stand tall and proud on the seat of the chair. Your woman will have to do a headstand and push up and down.

Difficulty 10/10 *Coitus uninterruptus is very hard. It'll take all your balancing skills not to topple like an old fell oak. Try it during the Queen's speech at Christmas.*

10. PRAYING MANTIS

Aim Every now and then you'll want to take a different perspective on life from the chair. This position offers you a little adventure.

Method Your girlfriend gets to relax in the traditional male seated position. You sit facing her, then tip back to watch the box upside-down. It's your woman's job to keep you "in".

Difficulty 7/10 *You'll have to have a pretty flexible back, and penis, for this one. It's perfect for stuff she likes which you find more interesting upside-down: Ellen, say, or The Shopping Channel.*

11. THE HAPPY TANDEM

Aim To enjoy a comfortable sit-down shag while not being too distracted from a mutually appreciated TV favourite.

Method Simple. You sit facing the TV. She sits facing the TV – only she's on your lap, riding you like a good 'un.

Difficulty 4/10 *The only major problem with The Happy Tandem is a tendency for you to slip out should your lady jump up during, say, a particularly exciting episode of Friends.*

12. POSTCARD FROM THE EDGE

Aim To gain maximum deep penetration during a time of heightened excitement.

Method With your buttocks on the edge of the chair, you pleasure your girlfriend in the traditional doggy style as she kneels, table-like, in front of you.

Difficulty 3/10 *For the first time you'll have to concentrate a little. This can be done during edge-of-the-seat action blockbusters like Raiders Of The Lost Ark, the Star Wars trilogy and Beethoven's Second.*

1 NO ITEMISED BILLS Paying for a meal with your mistress on credit, let alone lingerie, flowers or assorted love gifts, is tantamount to leaving a note to your wife that says: "Ha ha ha, I'm getting it somewhere else, loser." At least, it is when she steams open your Visa statement. Always use cash, and destroy all receipts.

2 AVOID THE PHONE If you have to ring home from your mistress's, dial 141 beforehand so your wife can't trace the call. Excessive mobile bills will arouse suspicion, as will hiding them altogether. If you have an itemised phone bill, have it changed it to an "all in" bill. And only a fool would ring his mistress from home – but if you do, dial a mate's number afterwards, in case your partner presses redial.

"You left your bloody knickers in my Escort again!"

If you're going to cheat on your partner, remember these ten golden rules

A BIT ON THE SIDE...

3 ALWAYS TAKE TAXIS When visiting your other woman, avoid taking the car. You'd be amazed how many of your wife's friends will happen to pass her flat and recognise the number plate. If leaving the car at home is even more suspicious, drive it round to a friend or a long-stay car park and take a taxi from there. If you're daft enough to entertain her in your own home, insist that she does the same.

4 DON'T LET HER WEAR PERFUME You must impress on your other lover that she must be scentless from now on, even though it goes against the grooming instinct of a woman. The slightest hint of girlish body-spray on your clothes endows a suspicious woman with the sensory detectors of a blood-hound. That also goes for lipstick, foundation and mascara.

5 CONTROL ALL SMELLS The smell of sex lingers longer than the scent of burnt rubber. Scrub yourself violently, and keep the soap you use at your mistress's. If you've pretended you're out with the lads, always stop at a pub on the way home to pick up the unmistakable stink of beer and fags on your clothes.

6 NEVER TOUCH HER IN PUBLIC However crazy you are about your "other" girlfriend, never even hold her hand when crossing the road. That will be the moment your wife's best mate sees you and takes a mental forensic photograph. Don't hold her hand over a restaurant table, don't brush hair out of her face at an office party, and never, ever kiss her in public. If you're not seen touching, she can be a colleague, a cousin, an old schoolfriend – but never your concubine.

7 DON'T CONFIDE IN FRIENDS The desire to boast about your studly prowess, or even seek advice, is where you could get found out. The minute your mate knows about your activities, so, potentially, does every one of his friends. And their friends. And soon, the only person who doesn't know will be your wife. Choose one confidante, who doesn't know your wife or mistress, and only ask him to lie for you when it's unavoidable. And tell no one else.

8 BE PREPARED TO DOUBLE-UP Obviously, your partner doesn't know you spent the afternoon thrusting joyfully into another woman. So she might, at some point, suggest you have sex. Particularly if she's feeling neglected. If you turn her down too often you might as well strap a sign to your head saying "all shagged out". Which means you're going have to overcome your tiredness and guilt, and get down to it once again.

9 DON'T SMARTEN UP If you've always been something of a slob, a sudden interest in personal grooming will set alarm bells jangling. A new aftershave, a poncy shower gel, or doubling the time you spend in front of the mirror fiddling with your hair are all suspicious. And developing a new pattern or attempting to introduce new sexual positions into your well-worn repertoire looks iffy, however tempting.

10 ALWAYS HAVE AN EXPLANATION The worst thing you can do is arrive home at 2am, covered in lipstick and without an excuse. If you were to say "Jesus, the guys dragged me to this gay club, there was some bloody drag queen got me up on stage" convincingly, having checked the existence of such a club in the local listings paper, you may have a chance. If you say "Buh, duh, buh – it's not how it seems", you're a dead man. Because if you don't verify your story, by God she will.

REX

1. You come home from an office party two hours late. What does she do?
a) Rolls over in bed, muttering "about flaming time, stop-out".
b) Gets up to greet you and smilingly asks how it went.
c) Stands amidst your suits, their arms and legs shredded into ribbons, and hisses: "It'll be you next time, alright?"

2. How does PMT affect her?
a) She groans about it, clutching her head, crying irrationally and accidentally breaking things.
b) She takes her Evening Primrose and remains as sweet as ever.
c) She goes into the kitchen, takes the plates from the cupboard and hurls them at you, screaming: "It's all a fucking conspiracy, and you're at the head of it, you bastard."

3. You take her to your parents. What's her opening gambit?
a) "Alright, Mr and Mrs Thing? Nice to meet you."
b) "Geoffrey and Pauline! Your garden's a blaze of colour, it looks stunning!"
c) "I'm not too good with families. See, I never had one. At least, not after the *accident*."

4. If she was going to commit a crime, which of these offences might it be?
Nicking bread to feed a starving family; going half-fare on the bus; taking illegal drugs; speeding on the motorway. Or...
Slashing her prettier sister's face with a razor; slicing off your penis with a kitchen knife; burning down a house because it contains bad memories; stalking a famous pop star and posting him turds when he fails to respond.

5. You suddenly go off sex. What does she assume?
a) You're getting old and feeble.
b) You're getting terribly tired, poor darling.
c) You're getting it from her sister, five times a day.

6. You're planning a US trip. Where would she like to go?
a) New York: a funky, vibrant cultural melting pot.
b) Boston: high-brow, historic,

beautiful buildings.
c) Roswell: because maybe you can be the ones who prove those alien corpses were no hoax.

7. She doesn't like sleeping alone. Why?
a) Because you warm the bed nicely and you're a decent shag.
b) Because she loves to cuddle you all night long.
c) Because night is when The Visions come, and strange forces pin her to the bed.

8. What did she get told off for at school?
a) Chatting in class and messing about instead of concentrating.
b) Being a sneak and telling tales.
c) Terrifying the class by appearing to go into trances and contacting their dead relatives.

9. She doesn't like you cutting your hair. Why?
a) Because you look like a skinhead wanker when it's short.
b) Because you look so romantic when it's longer – like a poet.
c) Because each hair has a soul, and they'll die, screaming in agony, if you hurt them.

10. You feel like you're being watched. Why does she think this is?
a) Because you're doing 90 down the motorway and there are flashing blue lights up ahead.
b) Because girls always look at you – you're so handsome.
c) Because your Red Indian spirit guide, Eagle Claw, is behind you.

11. What were the last words her ex said to her?
a) "Yeah, well you can fuck off, too, alright?"
b) "I hope we can still be friends."
c) "Please put the knife down. Slooowly..."

12. What did she hate most about her ex?
a) His stupid mates and their blokey conversations.
b) His long hours at work.
c) His desire to see other people. *Any* other people.

13. If you got married, how would she like to do it?
a) In the Elvis Chapel at Las Vegas, watched by admiring tourists.
b) In her local church, watched

by loving family and friends.
c) In a wood, watched by the spirit of Lilith, The Great Witch.

14. Who is her best friend?
a) A woman she met at work.
b) A woman she's known since school.
c) Her pet rock.

15. Her friend turns up an hour late for a shopping trip. What does she say?
a) "Blimey, you old slapper – what kept you?"
b) "Not to worry, the traffic can be dreadful."
c) "If you hate me, just fucking say so, alright?"

16. What kind of birthday celebration would she enjoy?
a) You hire a club, Judge Jules, and provide many crates of champagne for her 200 mates.
b) A trip to the theatre with a couple of friends.
c) Dancing naked with 13 women atop Pendle Hill at full moon.

17. Which of these incidents would make her consider chucking you?
Sleeping with another woman; insulting her mother; failing to turn up for a date; getting offensively pissed at her works do; booking a holiday without telling her; taking too long in the bathroom every morning; forgetting to leave the toilet seat down; listening to music too loud; arranging to see a friend; failing to turn over the end of the Sellotape; hanging your underpants the wrong way round to dry; owning a blue shirt; buying the wrong kind of loaf; smiling.

18. Do you feel dangerously vulnerable when asleep?
Yes/No

19. You feel unwell. Do you search her handbag for clues?
Yes/No

20. Are you afraid to use the telephone in case she's bugged it?
Yes/No

21. A man seems to be following you. Do you assume she's employed him?
Yes/No

22. How do your friends react when she accompanies you to the pub?
a) Cheery smiles, back-slapping, pints all round.
b) Some slight eye-rolling, but generally welcoming.

KOBAL

YOU DATING A NUTTER?

Loonies: good fun at parties, always a source of amusing stories. But waking up next to one is a whole different ball game. Face facts – is your girl barking?

c) They go into a huddle to thrash out a credible excuse for leaving immediately.

23. You leave her for another woman. What would be her idea of reasonable revenge?
a) Throwing paint all over your car and generally bad-mouthing you round town.
b) Eventually being happy with someone better-looking and richer than you.
c) Death, administered by her with a horsewhip after three days of you hanging upside-down while being jeered at by the townsfolk.

24. You mention that her mother must have been beautiful when she was young. Next time you see her mum, what is she like?
a) The same as usual – slightly grumpy and harrassed.
b) She smiles warmly at you, thrilled by the compliment.
c) Recovering in hospital from having acid thrown in her face.

25. You let her down after promising to take her out. Next day, what do you receive through the post?
a) A terse note saying "Thanks a bunch".
b) A card saying "Let's put our differences behind us" over a picture of a sunset.
c) A dead rat, positively crawling with maggots.

26. She's crying at her sister's wedding. Why?

No one got between Beryl and her Immac

a) Because the groom's a bit of an arse, and she's worried.
b) Because it's so sweet, and she wants to get married too.
c) Because weddings are nothing less than legalised prostitution, and now her own sister's become a whore.

27. When did she first say she loved you?
a) After a few months, when she was pissed.
b) After a few weeks, while walking in the countryside.
c) After five minutes. Then she was sick on your shoes.

28. Tick the things she experienced in her teens:
Heroin; the Bangkok Hilton; S&M; Araldite fumes; Alaistair Crowley's teachings; Holloway; how firing a gun feels; how ripping out entrails with a hunting knife feels; a stomach pump; a hardcore porn shoot; Satanic abuse.

29. You meet her from work. What does she say?
a) "Oh, I was just going for a pint with Sue."
b) "Oh darling, how thoughtful."
c) "For Christ's sake, don't let them see you – they don't know who I really am."

30. She buys a car with blacked-out windows. Why?
a) She wants to feel like she's a pop star.
b) Because the sun gives her migraines.
c) So that she can stalk more efficiently.

31. Five years on, you see her with a child. Who's is it?
a) It's her niece.
b) It's hers.
c) It's stolen.

32. You're rowing in public. What does she do?
a) Stand up and say "I'm

leaving" in a fairly loud voice.
b) Crouch down and say "Not here" in a whisper.
c) Stand on a chair and shout: "Right, who fucking agrees with me?"

33. Does she sleepwalk?
Yes/No

34. Have all her friends moved away?
Yes/No

35. Does she believe Diana was murdered by Mossad?
Yes/No

36. Does she think the world will end in our lifetime?
Yes/No

37. Which of these has she ingested in the same night?
Tequila; Special Brew; ecstasy; cocaine; crack; speed; Creme de Menthe; poppers; GBH; LSD; a bouncer's bodily fluids.

38. What would be a good reason for her to hit you?
a) You hit her.
b) There's no good reason.
c) Your face was in the way.

39. She asks you to her church meeting. What do you expect to find?
a) Vaguely Christian youngsters with guitars.
b) Quiet elderly people, praying.
c) Two thousand brides and grooms chanting their wedding vows to a hologram.

40. Does she ever refer to a mysterious past incident that ended in tragedy?
Yes/No

**41. If she ever had a tattoo,

what would it be?**
a) A rose, nestled on her shoulder-blade.
b) A transfer of a swallow on her arm.
c) A galleon in full sail covering her entire torso.

42. What's her view on California's "Death Row"?
a) If you can't do the time, don't do the crime
b) Horribly barbaric – thank God we don't have it over here.
c) She looks forward to their letters every day.

43. Has she ever rung you at four in the morning in hysterics for any reason other than bereavement?
Yes/No

44. Has she ever tied a man to the bed and gone home?
Yes/No

45. Has she ever toyed with becoming a prostitute?
Yes/No

46. Has she ever started a row about nothing what-soever, and ended it sobbing "I'd rather be dead than endure this hell"?
Yes/No

47. Where'll she live when old?
a) Near her daughter, where she'll pootle to the shops and back.
b) Surrounded by grandchildren.
c) She'll be shuffling through urine-stained newspapers to feed liver to her 18 cats.

48. You are talking to a girl in the pub when she arrives. How does she greet her?
a) "Hello, who are you?"
b) "Hello, can I get you a drink?"
c) With a stinging slap.

49. You're about to go to a party. How do you feel?
a) Mildly excited at the thought of mates and beer.
b) Proud that she's on your arm.
c) Queasy with fear regarding what she might do.

50. She's giving you a blow-job. Why are you uneasy?
a) She might stop.
b) She might not want to do it.
c) She might bite it off.

SCORING

■ Question four: none, B; first four, A; second four, C.
■ Question 17: none, B; one to five, A; six or more, C.
■ Question 28: C for each tick.
■ Question 37: none, B; one to two, A; three or more, C.

MOSTLY A She isn't remotely a lunatic. Sane, a good laugh, pleasant to know and slightly grumpy – that's your girl. There's no chance she'll do anything loopy, because she's experimented enough in the past to know that being mad's no fun: you only attract other nutters and spend every night puking violently following substance abuse. While relatively vengeful, she's well within the bounds of normality; she won't strike until she's harmed, at least. She may have a couple of lunatic exes, but thinks you're pretty sane – no room for crazies in this girl's life.

MOSTLY B This woman is so sane she makes Jane Asher look like Darth Vader. But in fact, no one can be so decent, good and down to earth without a few skeletons rattling the wardrobe at night. What has she done that she feels the need to compensate for with endless calm and patience? What makes her every day an act of atonement? You'll never know, because she's not a lunatic – but there's something going on in the dark recesses of her brain, for sure.

MOSTLY C Mad. This woman is barking. How you came to be involved with her is too worrying to contemplate, but now that you are you'd better start figuring how you're going to leave with your genitals intact. She's left destruction and exhaustion behind her, so before you lose all your friends to her insane hatreds and your dignity to her randomly-thrown punches, it's time to go. But better wait 'til she's asleep.